United States
Department of
Agriculture

Forest Service

**Northern
Research Station**

General Technical
Report NRS-19

Natural Disturbance and Stand Development Principles for Ecological Forestry

Jerry F. Franklin
Robert J. Mitchell
Brian J. Palik

Abstract

Foresters use natural disturbances and stand development processes as models for silvicultural practices in broad conceptual ways. Incorporating an understanding of natural disturbance and stand development processes more fully into silvicultural practice is the basis for an ecological forestry approach. Such an approach must include 1) understanding the importance of biological legacies created by a tree regenerating disturbance and incorporating legacy management into harvesting prescriptions; 2) recognizing the role of stand development processes, particularly individual tree mortality, in generating structural and compositional heterogeneity in stands and implementing thinning prescriptions that enhance this heterogeneity; and 3) appreciating the role of recovery periods between disturbance events in the development of stand complexity. We label these concepts, when incorporated into a comprehensive silvicultural approach, the "three-legged stool" of ecological forestry. Our goal in this report is to review the scientific basis for the three-legged stool of ecological forestry to provide a conceptual foundation for its wide implementation.

INTRODUCTION

Foresters use natural disturbances and stand development processes as models for silvicultural practices in broad conceptual ways. For example, even-aged harvest prescriptions are often described as analogs for stand-replacement disturbances, such as intense wildfires or windstorms (Smith et al. 1996). Individual tree and group selection practices are modeled on patterns of disturbance and mortality that involve the death of individual or small groups of trees within otherwise intact stands. Silvicultural thinning (from below) is designed to capture density-dependent mortality before it occurs naturally. Hence, disturbance regimes and stand development processes are the conceptual foundation for the core of silviculture. However, silviculturalists have only recently begun to look beyond the type, intensity, and scale of disturbances to the specific ecological conditions created by natural disturbances and stand development and to more fully incorporate these conditions into silvicultural prescriptions (Kohm and Franklin 1997).

Incorporating an understanding of natural disturbance and stand development processes more fully into silvicultural practice is the basis for an ecological forestry approach. Implementing such an approach successfully requires that prescriptions be founded on a conceptual basis that links stand disturbance and dynamics to the development and maintenance of ecological complexity of stands, as expressed in structure, composition, and heterogeneity of these features in space and time. The implementation and expression of ecological forestry concepts will vary in practice based upon specific goals for management, characteristics of tree species and ecosystems, variation in starting conditions of stands and sites, and landscape context. However, our premise in this report is that some fundamental principles for ecological forestry transcend systems, conditions, objectives, and context, and can be applied in varying degrees in virtually all settings where melding of ecological and economic goals is an objective.

JERRY F. FRANKLIN *is a professor of ecosystem analysis at the College of Forest Resources, University of Washington, Seattle, WA.*

ROBERT J. MITCHELL *is a senior scientist at the Joseph E. Jones Ecological Research Center in Newton, GA.*

BRIAN J. PALIK *is an ecologist and project leader with the U.S. Forest Service, Northern Research Station.*

Three fundamental principles have emerged from research on natural disturbance regimes and stand development processes, which form the basis of an ecological forestry approach. These include 1) understanding the importance of biological legacies created by a tree-regenerating disturbance and incorporating legacy management into harvesting prescriptions; 2) recognizing the role of stand development processes, particularly individual tree mortality, in generating structural and compositional heterogeneity in stands and implementing thinning prescriptions that enhance this heterogeneity; and 3) appreciating the role of recovery periods between disturbances in the development of stand complexity. We label these concepts, when incorporated into a comprehensive silvicultural approach, the "three-legged stool" of ecological forestry (Fig. 1).

Our goal in this report is to review the scientific basis for the three-legged stool of ecological forestry to provide a conceptual foundation for its wide implementation. Specifically, we 1) review the concept of biological legacies; 2) present a conceptual model of natural disturbance regimes focused on the types and amounts of biological legacies they create, and contrast natural disturbances with their regeneration harvest counterparts with respect to biological legacies; 3) review tree mortality processes during stand development with respect to generating structural heterogeneity and contrast stand development mortality with silvicultural thinning for their respective effects on heterogeneity; 4) review the importance of recovery periods for generating stand complexity and contrast this with the implementation of rotation periods; and 5) provide principles and guidelines for incorporating natural disturbance and development concepts into silvicultural prescriptions that sustain or restore ecological complexity.

Sidebar 1.—The Three-Legged Stool of Ecological Forestry

A useful analogy for ecological forestry is a three-legged stool (Fig. 1). For the stool to function effectively each leg must contribute support to the seat. Remove one leg and the stool might support weight in a precariously balanced position for a time, but eventually the stool will fall. Remove two legs and it will fall sooner. By analogy, ecological forestry (the seat of the stool) depends on each of its three principles (legs of the stool) to fully succeed. These legs or principles for management include (1) retention of biological legacies at harvest; (2) intermediate treatments that enhance stand heterogeneity; and (3) allowances for appropriate recovery periods between regeneration harvests.

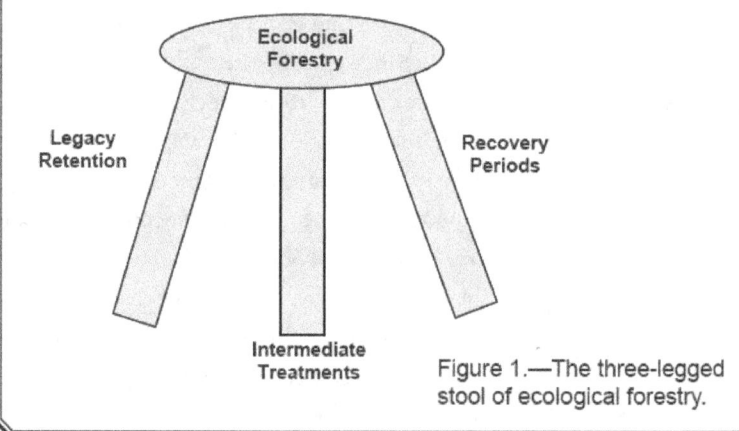

Figure 1.—The three-legged stool of ecological forestry.

BIOLOGICAL LEGACIES

Biological legacies as a concept emerged from studies that demonstrate that natural disturbances—even disturbances as intense as the Mount St. Helens eruptions (Franklin et al. 2000, Franklin and MacMahon 2000)—rarely create the simple and homogeneous environment that is sometimes imagined and often emulated with even-aged silviculture (Fig. 2). While disturbances may dramatically disrupt the ecosystem and kill trees, limited amounts of organic matter are actually consumed or removed (Franklin et al. 1997). Much of the residual organic matter persists as structures—such as standing dead trees (snags) and tree boles and other woody debris on the ground—that provide critical habitat for organisms and fill other important functional roles in the ecosystem (e.g., Harmon et al. 2004, Hunter 1999, Maser et al. 1988). In addition, many live mature trees, seedlings, and seeds survive intense disturbances. As with

Figure 2.—Biological legacies left after natural disturbances including: a) understory plant communities, tree seedling banks, snags and logs after volcanic eruption, Mount St. Helens, Washington; b) understory plant communities, tree seedling and sapling banks, and large volumes of down tree boles after stand-replacement wind disturbances, Bull Run River drainage, Mount Hood National Forest, Oregon; c) snags and associated woody debris after stand-replacement fire, Yosemite National Park, California.

many ecological constructs, the concept of biological legacies is not wholly new; rather, it is a revision and elaboration of Frederic Clements' concept of organic "residuals" proposed nearly 100 years ago (Clements 1916).

Biological legacies are defined as the organisms, organic matter (including structures), and biologically created patterns that persist from the pre-disturbance ecosystem and influence recovery processes in the post-disturbance ecosystem (Franklin et al. 2000). Legacies occur in varied forms and densities, depending upon the nature of both the disturbance and the forest ecosystem (Table 1).

Biological legacies play important roles in ecosystem reorganization and recovery following disturbance (Franklin et al. 2000, Franklin and MacMahon 2000). A generalized function of legacies is that of "lifeboating" or perpetuating genotypes and species *in situ*, which is particularly relevant to conserving biological diversity within heavily disturbed forest ecosystems (Lindenmayer and Franklin 2002). Specific mechanisms by which biological legacies "lifeboat" biological diversity include the following:

- Perpetuating plant species, as surviving immature or mature individuals or as reproductive structures, such as seeds, spores, or vegetative parts with sprouting capability

- Perpetuating biota by providing habitat, supplying energy and nutrients, and by modifying microclimatic conditions

- Providing habitat for recolonizing organisms, primarily by structurally enriching the developing young stand

- Improving connectivity in the landscape for some organisms by providing protective cover within the disturbed area

Table 1.—Categories and examples of biological legacies

Legacy category	Examples
Organisms	Sexually mature and intact live trees
	Tree reproduction (seedling and sapling banks)
	Vegetatively reproducing parts (e.g., roots)
	Seed banks
	Shrub, herb, bryophyte species
	Mature and immature animals and microbes
Organic matter	Fine litter
	Particulate material
Organically derived structures	Standing dead trees
	Downed trees and other coarse woody debris
	Root wads and pits from uprooted trees
Organically derived patterns	Soil chemical, physical, microbial properties
	Forest understory composition and distribution

These roles are particularly prominent where a large and intense (i.e., stand replacement) disturbance has taken place, but they also occur with smaller disturbances, such as within midsize to large canopy gaps in an otherwise intact stand.

A major part of the lifeboating function is typically provided by larger biological structures that persist following a disturbance, such as live trees, snags, and downed boles. These structures sustain organisms in the post-disturbance environment by providing necessary habitat (e.g., nesting sites and hiding cover) and energy, especially right after the disturbance. Live green plants have particular importance in sustaining high-quality energy flows to belowground organisms and food webs, as well as to aboveground herbivores. For example, residual trees in retention harvests in Douglas-fir forests (Fig. 3) are associated with increased diversity of ectomycorrhizal fungi, which are important for seedling nutrition and survival (Louma et al. 2006). Residual structures also modify microclimate, often bringing it within the acceptable environmental range for organisms to survive.

Figure 3.—Legacy Douglas-fir left after a retention harvest in the Cascade Range.

Table 2.—Biological legacies associated with wind, fire, and bark beetle disturbances

Legacy	Wind Tree	Wind Gap	Wind Stand	Fire* Tree	Fire* Gap	Fire* Stand	Beetle Tree	Beetle Gap	Beetle Stand
Live, mature trees	NA	Few/Absent	Few/Absent	NA	Few	Few	NA	Species dependent	Species dependent
Seedling bank	Possible	Possible	Possible	No	No/Rare	Rare	Possible	Possible	Possible
Intact understory	Possible	Yes	Yes	No	Rare	Rare	Possible	Yes	Yes
Snags	NA	Few	Few	Yes	Abundant	Abundant	Yes	Abundant	Abundant
Logs	Yes	Abundant	Abundant	No	No	Common	No	No	No
Uproots	Yes	Abundant	Abundant	No	No	No	No	No	No
Mineral seedbed	Yes	Yes	Yes	Yes	Yes	Abundant	No	No	No

*Fire at the tree and gap scales is largely surface fire that spreads through a stand (with or without crowning) and may kill individual or small groups of trees.

Compositional legacies can be as important as structural legacies with regard to many aspects of ecosystem function (Palik and Engstrom 1999). Compositional legacies include the variety of organisms that survive a disturbance including trees, other plants, fungi, and animals. In forest ecosystems, tree-derived legacies are important in facilitating survival of organisms other than trees, but we must not forget that these organisms themselves play important roles in re-establishing a diverse and functional forest ecosystem (Dale et al. 2005). Both structural and compositional legacies may also play a role in sustaining natural disturbance regimes. As an example, overstory tree legacies provide fuel for fire in systems that depend on fire, such as the longleaf pine (*Pinus palustris* Mill.), ponderosa pine (*Pinus ponderosa* Laws.), and Great Lakes pine ecosystems (Allen et al. 2002, Rebertus el al. 1989).

GENERAL MODEL OF DISTURBANCE AND LEGACY CREATION

Scientific understanding of disturbances and subsequent ecosystem recovery and development processes has increased dramatically during the last several decades. Several large and notable disturbances—the Mount St. Helens eruption of 1980 (Dale et al. 2005), the Yellowstone Fires of 1988 (Christensen et al. 1989), and Hurricanes Hugo (Walker et al. 1991) and Andrew (Pimm et al. 1994)—provided opportunities for ecosystem research teams to extend their studies of recovery processes to intensely disturbed ecosystems. Concurrently, there has been an increased understanding of the structural effects of smaller scale disturbance regimes and natural development processes in forest ecosystems (e.g., Frelich and Lorimer 1991; Gray and Spies 1996; Kneeshaw and Bergeron 1998; Runkle 1982, 1998).

Research on natural disturbances has largely emphasized variables such as the type, size, frequency, intensity, and impact of the disturbances (e.g., Pickett and White 1985, Turner et al. 1998). Disturbance scale has also received significant attention, including a scientific synthesis of the distinctive features and effects of large intense disturbances (Turner et al. 1998). Predicting ecosystem responses to disturbances, however, is best understood by considering not only patterns of destruction or consumption, but also patterns and types of what remains following the disturbance, i.e., biological legacies.

Our general disturbance model incorporates scale and disturbance agent as the primary considerations in predicting kind, quantity, and spatial pattern of biological legacies (Table 2). Other widely discussed disturbance regime descriptors, i.e., intensity and frequency, are not treated directly, but are implicit in consideration of scale and agents.

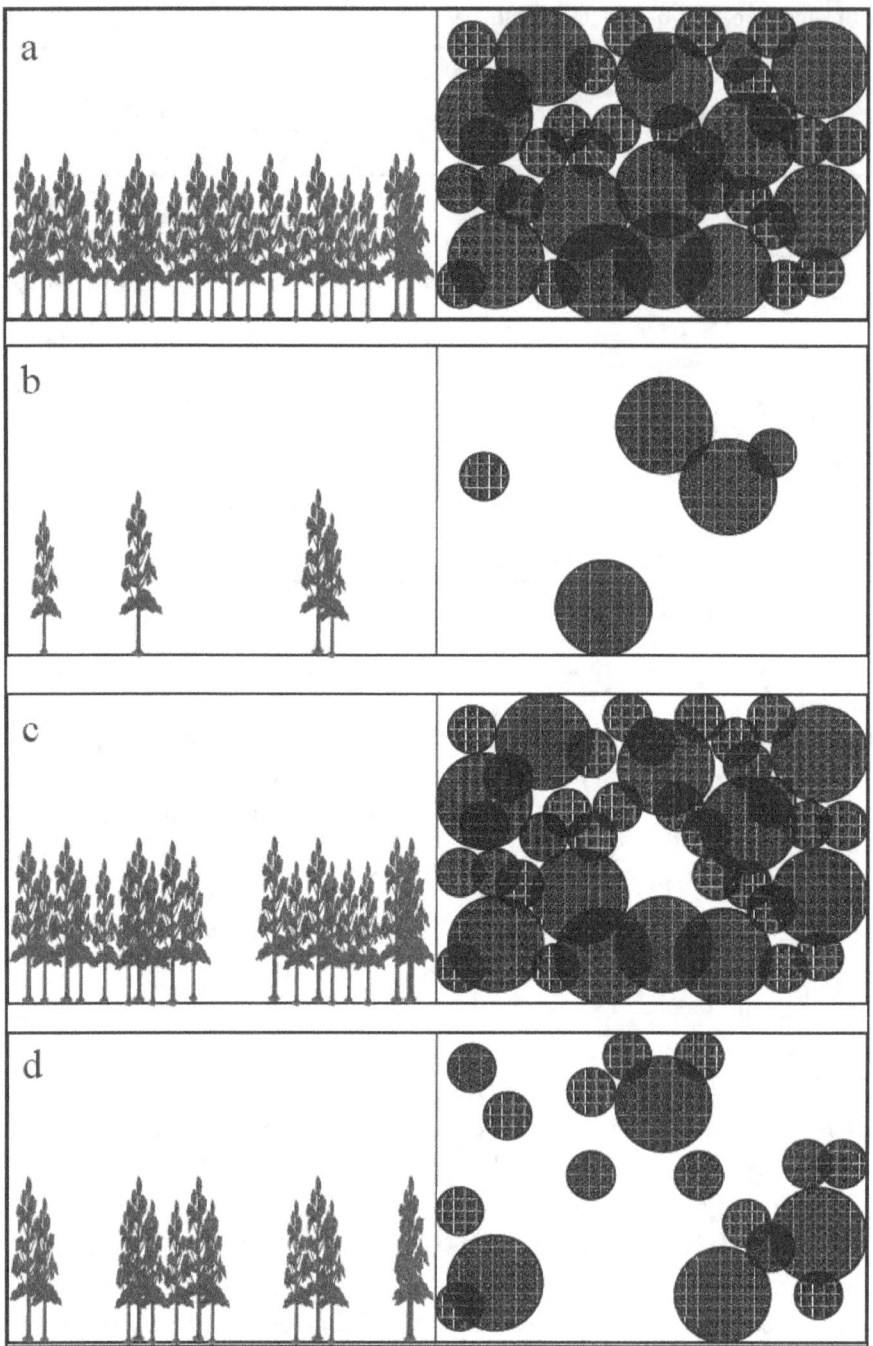

Figure 4.-Conceptual representation of spatial scale and distribution of overstory disturbance within a stand: (a) mature forest; (b) stand-replacement disturbance; (c) gap-scale disturbance; (d) partial canopy disturbance.

Disturbance Scale

Spatial scale of dominant tree mortality is one dimension of our model of tree-regenerating disturbance (Table 2). Disturbances are scaled from those involving individuals, to groups of overstory trees, and, finally, to large-scale mortality events, commonly described as stand-replacement disturbances. This gradient in size of individual disturbance events is correlated with proportion of the remaining intact forest and with degree of heterogeneity of structure and composition. Tree-scale and gap-scale mortality events leave the forest largely intact such that the forest matrix still dominates the post-disturbance environment (Fig. 4). Stand-level mortality events, on the other hand, destroy the dominant forest cover and shift the matrix to an open post-disturbance environment (Fig. 4). A condition intermediate to these two extremes results when multiple tree or gap events occur simultaneously (heavy, but partial canopy disturbance), leaving a stand that contains similar amounts of both open and intact canopy conditions (Fig. 4).

Stand-replacement events will generally homogenize (in a relative sense) the post-disturbance tree population structure of a stand by providing conditions for establishment or release of a new tree cohort and generating abundant coarse woody debris. Tree-scale and gap-scale events, on the other hand, tend to create or perpetuate stand structural heterogeneity, although in greater degrees with gap-scale events. Heavy partial canopy disturbance results in a high degree of structural heterogeneity and provides conditions for both new cohort establishment and release of residual trees (Fajvan and Seymour 1993).

Disturbance Agent

Disturbance agent is the other important dimension of tree-regenerating disturbances that directly affects biological legacies (Table 2). We use fire, wind, and bark beetles to exemplify the effect of disturbance agent on biological legacies because these are common agents and relate to disturbance regimes in many well-known forest types. Other agents of disturbance, while not discussed in detail here, also create legacies (Sidebar 2). Wind, fire, and bark beetles can kill trees across a range of spatial scales, from individual trees to entire stands, and these disturbance agents contrast greatly in their resultant biological legacies, irrespective of the scale of overstory tree mortality (Table 2).

Wind

Many forest types have a primary disturbance regime defined by wind-created gaps; even more forests incorporate this as a "secondary" regime (as discussed later). Legacies within wind- generated gaps typically include numerous boles on the forest floor and some large live trees and snags in larger gaps (Table 2). Cohorts of tree seedlings and saplings or seedling banks are often present, sometimes in high densities; these regeneration

banks are typically referred to as advance regeneration by foresters. Understory vegetation and seed banks are typically left intact, except around the uprooted area and where they are buried beneath boles and other debris. Exposed mineral soil typically is limited to areas influenced by uprooting, i.e., tree-fall pits and mounds, which are also important structural legacies.

North American forest types characterized by a wind-gap disturbance regime include Pacific Coast rainforests of western hemlock (*Tsuga heterophylla* (Raf.) Sarg.*)*, western redcedar (*Thuja plicata* Donn ex D. Don), Sitka spruce (*Picea sitchensis* (Bong.) Carr.) and Pacific silver fir (*Abies amabilis* (Dougl. ex Loud.) Dougl. ex Forbes) (Lertzman et al. 1996); northern hardwood forests of the Great Lakes and New England regions (Frelich and Lorimer 1991); and mid-Atlantic and southern hardwood forest ecosystems (Runkle 1982). In temperate South America, the lenga (*Nothofagus pumilio* (Poepp et Endl.) Krasser) forests of Tierra del Fuego provide an excellent example of a forest with a wind-gap disturbance regime (Arroyo et al. 1996, Rebertus et al. 1997).

Wind-generated disturbances at larger spatial scales (e.g., hurricanes, typhoons, straight-line winds, and tornadoes) are similar to wind-gap disturbances in the nature of biological legacies they produce (Table 2). Structural

Figure 5.—A stand of blowndown, jackstrawed (bent), and surviving red pine after an intense windstorm on the Huron-Manistee National Forest, Michigan. Photo credit: Linda Haugen, USDA Forest Service, www.forestryimages.org.

legacies are primarily downed boles with some snags and a few larger live trees (e.g., Foster and Boose 1992, Palik and Robl 1999, Peterson and Pickett 1995). Some snags often persist, probably because they have less surface area (i.e., no canopy), providing less purchase for winds. In many temperate and tropical hardwood forests, broken, bent, and partially uprooted trees have the capacity to re-sprout, even though they are no longer part of a dominant overstory (Foster et al. 1997, Walker et al. 1991); these damaged but live trees are an important structural legacy of the disturbance. The understory of affected stands remains largely intact, except for areas disrupted by uprooting or located directly under boles; hence, seed and seedling banks and understory plants are a major legacy of stand-scale wind disturbance. A stand of windthrown or jackstrawed trees (Fig. 5) also protect pre-disturbance and post-disturbance seedlings and other understory plants from browsing animals (Franklin and Dyrness 1973, Sharpe 1956).

Intense windstorms, including hurricanes, are an occasional disturbance for temperate hardwood forests in eastern North America (Canham and Loucks 1984, Foster and Boose 1992), in subtropical and tropical hardwood forests in the Caribbean region

and, occasionally, in pine forests of the southeastern Coastal Plain (Myers and Van Lear 1998). Intense windstorms also periodically disturb areas of conifer forests along the Pacific Coast from northern California to Alaska. Portions of the Pacific Northwest dominated by Douglas-fir (*Pseudotsuga menziesii* (Mirb.) Franco var. *menziesii*) forests are much better known for their stand-replacement fire regimes, but both large-scale and more localized stand-replacement wind events do occur as evidenced by the 1962 Columbus Day windstorm (Orr 1963). Infrequent, but intense windstorms are also important in the Great Lakes region (Canham and Loucks 1984, Frelich and Lorimer 1991, Palik and Robl 1999, Reich et al. 2001).

Fire

Fire kills overstory trees at either small (tree and gap) or large (stand) scales, but produces comparable legacies at all scales (Table 2). Typical legacies of fire include a high density of snags and, sometimes, down boles on the forest floor, but relatively few large live trees if it is truly a stand-replacement disturbance. However, some large trees typically survive even intense fires, as exemplified by such diverse forest types as jack pine (*Pinus banksiana* Lamb.) in the Lake States (Abrams 1984) and Douglas-fir on the Pacific Coast (Spies and Franklin 1991) (Fig. 6). As with all events that leave standing, dead, overstory trees, snags created by fire will eventually disintegrate to provide coarse woody debris on the ground.

Understory seedling and seed banks, understory plants, and organic layers on the soil surface are all affected by fire; however, some understory trees and plants typically survive either because of variable fire intensity or adaptations to fire, or both (Jacqmain et al. 1999). A tree seed bank may also persist as a result of ecological adaptations (serotinous cones) or fortuitous survival of portions of a current seed crop in the canopy (Larson and Franklin 2005). Abundant mineral soil seedbeds are an important legacy of fire disturbances.

Gap-scale stand openings are often part of a frequent, low to moderate intensity fire regime, as is characteristic of southeastern longleaf pine forests (Palik and Pederson 1996), some Great Lakes eastern white pine (*Pinus strobus* L.) and red pine (*Pinus resinosa* Ait.) forests (Heinselman 1973), and many ponderosa pine forests (Franklin and Van Pelt 2004). In these systems, surface fires occasionally crown, killing patches of overstory trees and creating gaps in the process.

Figure 6.—Individual Douglas-fir and western larch (*Larix occidentalis* Nutt.) trees survived this intense, stand-replacement fire on the Colville National Forest, Washington.

Fires may actually cover a large area, but kill few overstory trees and thus generate few gaps. In southern longleaf pine woodlands, many understory and ground cover plants are adapted to regular burning (Kirkman et al. 2004), while many potential canopy species, such as oaks, survive fire, but do not grow tall (Jacqmain et al. 1999). In some of the forest types subject to this regime—such as longleaf pine—overstory tree mortality is caused primarily by lightning or bark beetles rather than by surface fires (Fig. 7; Palik and Pederson 1996), but these lighting strikes are an important ignition source for surface fires, which are fueled by pine needles and flammable grasses (Williamson and Black 1981).

Figure 7.—Dominant longleaf pines are susceptible to injury and mortality from lightning strikes, such as this tree at the Jones Ecological Research Center in southwest Georgia. Lightning strikes are important ignition sources for surface fires. Lightning injuries can induce declines in vigor in otherwise healthy trees, leading to attacks by various bark beetles.

Figure 8.—Competitive-exclusion phase in a 45-year-old Douglas-fir plantation on the Upper Cowlitz District of the Gifford Pinchot National Forest, Washington. Photo credit: Andrew J. Larson.

High intensity, stand-replacement fire is a common disturbance regime for many important forest types in North America. These include coastal Douglas-fir forests (Spies et al. 1988), jack pine and red pine forests in the Great Lakes region (Heinselman 1973, Van Wagner 1971), lodgepole pine (*Pinus contorta* Dougl. ex Loud.) forests throughout much of western North America (Romme and Knight 1981), and subalpine and boreal spruce (*Picea* spp.) forests in North America (Galipeau et al. 1997). Highly variable fire intensities are characteristic of these large fires; consequently, high levels of spatial heterogeneity in burn intensity and type and density of biological legacies are common. This heterogeneity is found at all spatial scales, from within stands to landscapes, resulting in patches of varying burn intensity as well as unburned patches.

Bark Beetles

Bark beetle disturbances can occur at a variety of spatial scales, with specifics depending upon the beetle and host species. The Douglas-fir bark beetle (*Dendroctonus pseudotsugae* Hopkins) typically kills small groups of mature to old Douglas-firs, producing a gap (Franklin et al. 2002). Similarly, western pine beetle (*D. brevicomis* LeConte) kills individual or small patches of ponderosa pine in old-growth stands (Johnson et al. 2003). Where extensive pure stands of host species exist, several species of bark beetles are capable of large-scale stand-replacement disturbances. Notable examples are the

southern pine beetle (*D. frontalis* Zimmermann) in plantations of southern pines (McNulty et al. 1998), the mountain pine beetle (*D. ponderosae* Hopkins) in young to mature stands of ponderosa pine and lodgepole pine as well as in extensive old-growth stands of lodgepole pine (Romme et al. 1986), and the spruce beetle (*D. rufipennis* (Kirby)) in spruce-dominated forests throughout subalpine and boreal forest regions in North America (Veblen et al. 1991). Snags and, eventually, boles and other coarse woody debris on the forest floor are primary biological legacies of beetle outbreaks (Table 2). Intact understory communities, including seedling and seed banks and undisturbed forest floors are also legacies.

Interactions between Disturbance Scales and Agent

Scale and agent can interact to determine the specifics of a disturbance regime. One of the most significant interactions involves forest types that are characterized by both stand-replacement events (wind, fire) and gap-scale events (wind, beetles). Forest developmental sequences initiated by catastrophic disturbances are invariably subject to gap-based disturbance processes that typically operate throughout stand development; the longer the developmental timespan, the more influential the gap-based processes become (Franklin et al. 2002).

Coastal Douglas-fir stands are a case in point. In these forests, time intervals between stand-replacement wildfires may exceed 400 years (Agee 1993, Franklin et al. 2002, Hemstrom and Franklin 1982). Assuming that succession begins with destruction of an old-growth forest stand, a spatially patchy, multi-aged stand is replaced with a relatively even-aged cohort of trees by the initiating disturbance. Where live-tree structures are concerned, the stand-replacement fire can be viewed as a homogenizing event, although it can create landscape-level heterogeneity (Delong and Kessler 2000). During the youthful competitive-exclusion stage of development, density-dependent competitive mortality among the young conifer cohort contributes further to structural homogeneity within the stand (Fig. 8), because the mortality is concentrated in smaller tree sizes and is most intense in the densest portions of the stands (Franklin et al. 2002). As the Douglas-fir cohort matures, mortality shifts to such density-independent agents as wind, bark

Table 3.—Biological legacies associated with common regeneration harvest methods as traditionally applied

	Method					
	Even-aged		Two-aged		Uneven-aged	
Legacy	Clearcut with site prep	Seed tree with site prep	Shelterwood with site prep[1]	Shelterwood with reserves and site prep	Group selection	Single-tree selection
Live, mature trees	No	Few/No	No	Yes	Few/No (in group)	n.a.
Seedling bank	No	No	Yes	Yes	Possible	Possible
Intact understory	No	No	No	Possible	Possible	Possible
Snags	No	No	No	No	No (in group)	n.a.
Logs	Few/No	Few/No	Few/No	Few/No	Few/No (in group)	No
Uproots	No	No	No	No	No	No
Mineral seedbed[2]	Yes	Yes	Yes	Yes	Possible	Possible

[1]Following final removal of overstory.
[2]Assuming ground-based harvesting.

beetles, and root and bole diseases, which affect trees in the largest diameter classes and are typically spatially aggregated. This shift in causes and patterns of mortality results in the development of canopy gaps within the stand and, consequently, regeneration and release of shade-tolerant associates, such as western hemlock and western redcedar. Hence, gap-based disturbances come to dominate within a maturing of the Douglas-fir forest sere and continue to do so until a stand-replacement event erases this spatially complex stand structure.

A similar interaction of disturbance scale and agent is seen in aspen ecosystems in the Great Lakes region of the United States. Many aspen (*Populus grandidentata* Michx., *P. tremuloides* Michx.) stands are characterized by largely single-cohort structure, initiating after stand-replacing disturbances, particularly fire or logging (Graham et al. 1963). As the stand matures, aspen begin to die from localized wind disturbance and disease, opening gaps that provide opportunities for establishment or release of later successional species, including tolerant northern hardwoods on richer sites or eastern white pine, white spruce (*Picea glauca* (Moench) Voss), and other conifers on poorer sites (Frelich and Reich 1995; Palik and Pregitzer 1993a, 1994). In either case, structurally complex, multi-cohort and mixed-species stands develop.

This pattern of gradual modification of homogenous, even-aged stands, by gap-level disturbance events appears to be repeated in most forest types subject to stand-replacement disturbances, whether initiated by fire or other agents of mortality. Some of these types may not reach the level of spatial complexity characteristic of old-growth stands, due to lack of longevity, limited tree growth potential, and insufficient intervals between stand-replacement disturbances. Nevertheless, the pattern whereby gap-based disturbances gradually modify the homogenizing influence of the stand-replacement event is common.

CONTRASTS BETWEEN NATURAL DISTURBANCES AND TRADITIONAL REGENERATION SYSTEMS

Biological legacies typically left after traditional regeneration harvest practices and those created by natural disturbances can be distinctly different. The contrasts can be significant whether silvicultural approaches involve even-aged, two-aged, or uneven-aged regeneration harvesting techniques (Table 3).

Stand-Replacement Disturbances vs. Even-Aged Management Systems

Clearcut, seed tree, and shelterwood are the standard even-aged regeneration approaches. In their purest forms,

Figure 9.—Significant legacies in the form of snags, fallen trees, and live residual trees are left after an intense windstorm on the Chequamegon-Nicolet National Forest in northern Wisconsin. The level of complexity in managed even-aged stands is substantially reduced relative to this condition.

they do not provide for any long-term retention of live or dead trees from the harvested stand (Table 3). Typically, overstory trees retained following a seed tree cut and an initial shelterwood harvest entries are eventually removed after successful establishment of regeneration (Smith et al. 1996). The option of retaining live trees indefinitely is explicitly mentioned only in seed tree cutting (Smith et al. 1996) and in modification of even-aged systems, i.e., clearcut or shelterwood with reserves.

The lack of significant structural legacies is a major difference between these traditional even-aged harvest methods and natural stand-replacement disturbances, whether by fire, wind, or insects. Most prominent among the missing legacies are remnant live trees, snags, and downed boles (Fig. 9), with associated pit and mounds in the case of windthrow. Stand-scale harvest disturbances also tend to homogenize subsequent stand structure

(Bergeron et al. 1999), whereas natural disturbances that occur at the stand-replacement scale typically generate substantial spatial heterogeneity of biological legacies (Eberhart and Woodard 1987).

Other important contrasts between stand-replacement disturbances and traditional even-aged silviculture relate to spatial and temporal patterns in regeneration (Sidebar 3) and differences in size and shape of openings. Clearcuts are often smaller and have simpler shapes than areas affected by stand-replacement disturbances (Bergeron et al. 2002, Seymour et al. 2002), unless they have been specifically designed to minimize visual impacts. Clearcut boundaries are also abrupt rather than feathered like boundaries of many natural disturbances.

Gap-Creating Disturbances vs. Uneven-Aged Management Systems

Single-tree selection and group selection are the traditional uneven-aged regeneration systems (Smith et al. 1996). Theoretically, selection practices are modeled closely on individual tree or gap-based natural disturbance regimes. In practice, these approaches can be highly formalized, such as where selection of trees to harvest is driven by efforts to create balanced diameter distributions (Sidebar 4), even though most natural stands fail to exhibit such regularity or balance (Matthews 1989, O'Hara 1996). The ecological problem with this approach is that most selection prescriptions remove different sizes of trees and in different spatial patterns than small-scale natural disturbances (Seymour and Hunter 1999), with significant consequences for biological legacies (Table 3).

As with even-aged management, multi-aged management regimes can also result in homogenizing of structure (Seymour and Hunter 1999). For example, traditional selection systems for northern hardwood ecosystems in the Great Lakes region effectively drive overstory composition to sugar maple (*Acer saccharum* Marsh.) dominance (Strong et al. 1997), whereas unmanaged mature and old-growth stands often support four or five species in abundance and 10 or more species in total (Curtis 1959).

Sidebar 3.—Pattern Legacies: Tree Regeneration after Stand-Scale Disturbance

Even-aged management regimes and natural stand-replacement disturbances can differ substantially in the dynamics of tree regeneration. Natural regeneration following wildfire is typically variable in time and space, depending upon such factors as proximity of seed sources and occurrence of large seed crops (e.g., Wahlenburg 1946) and heterogeneity of the fire, which can leave patches of advance regeneration intact. In such situations, establishment of dense tree regeneration and subsequent tree canopy closure may take many years or even decades (Tappeiner et al. 1997), particularly on sites where the environment is severe or which have been subjected to multiple burns (e.g., Franklin and Hemstrom 1981, Palik and Pregitzer 1991). In other cases, regeneration may occur quite rapidly following wildfire (e.g., Isaac and Meagher 1936, Larson and Franklin 2005). Establishment of regeneration by planting—as is often practiced with even-aged management regimes—is designed to consistently produce rapid and uniform re-establishment of forest cover. This difference in spatial and temporal patterns of regeneration, resulting from heterogeneity of fire and legacies (i.e., advance regeneration, seed sources, or site conditions) is a significant difference between natural and silvicultural stand-replacement disturbance.

Sidebar 4.—The B-D-q Method

Traditionally, selection systems (single-tree and group) are implemented quantitatively using the B-D-q method (O'Hara 2001). The structural outcomes of this approach differ in several significant ways from the outcomes of single-tree or gap-based natural canopy disturbances. With the B-D-q approach, a target residual basal area (B) and maximum diameter (D) are specified a priori, while the distribution of trees across diameter classes is determined by the diminution quotient (q), a value that reflects the ratio of the number of trees in diameter class a, to the number in diameter class a+1 (Smith et al. 1996). With this approach, the resultant diameter distribution is a negative exponential, often referred to as a reverse J distribution.

Specification of a target residual basal area is not necessarily in conflict with a natural disturbance-based approach to uneven-aged management; it is reasonable to expect a manager to select this target basal area based on an understanding of stand responses to disturbance and the silvics of component species. However, many natural canopy disturbances often result in substantial horizontal variation in stand structure including basal area and canopy openness. In contrast, selection systems based on the B-D-q method may deliberately or inadvertently minimize horizontal variation in stand structure in an attempt to reach a constant target basal area throughout the stand.

Both the selection of maximum tree diameters and q values have the potential to move stands structurally in directions having little or no natural analog. The theoretical goal of the q quotient is to create "balanced" all-aged stands that will sustain timber yield; that is, stands with uniform ratios between successive diameter distributions across the full range of diameters. In reality, there are few examples of natural forests that exhibit such balanced distributions (Matthews 1989).

In practice, when sustained yield is the goal, high q values are selected because they allow for greater numbers of smaller (regeneration) trees, relative to low q values. High q values also select against larger diameter trees. These larger trees, often the oldest in the stand, are the hallmark of multi-cohort, old-growth forests and should be retained in some reasonable abundance if managing for ecological objectives has primacy over, or even equal priority with, timber objectives.

It is not likely that this dilemma can be overcome through careful choice of a q value, as neither field research nor computer simulation has found a value that is relevant to both economic and ecological objectives (Hann and Bare 1979, O'Hara, 2001). More importantly, it has been shown that stable multi-cohort tree populations can be achieved by diameter distributions other than a negative exponential (Goff and West 1975, Goodburn and Lorimer 1999, James et al. 2004, Leak 1996, Lorimer and Frelich 1984). Simulations also suggest that a negative exponential distribution may not maximize yields or optimize economic returns (Adams and Ek 1974, Bare and Opalach 1988, Erickson et al. 1990, Kaya and Buongiorno 1989).

Individual Tree Selection

Typical individual tree selection contrasts significantly with tree-scale natural disturbances in terms of the types, amounts, and pattern of trees removed, and, the nature of resultant biological legacies (Table 3). For various reasons, most selection systems involve the systematic removal of at least some of the very large and old trees (Moser et al. 2002). Many of these trees are the most valuable from a timber perspective and are viewed as no longer contributing significantly to stand growth based on a presumption that large old trees are overmature and likely to die in the near future. Thus, their removal is driven more by economic, rather than ecological, considerations. However, studies of tree demography in many forest types and for many tree species show that large trees actually have lower rates of mortality—i.e., greater probability of survival—than smaller trees, at least until individuals get very large (Lorimer et al. 2001,

Monserud and Sterba 1999). Moreover, large old trees have tremendous ecological value, providing habitat in the form of cavities, deeply fissured bark, and large limbs.

In practice, most single-tree selection prescriptions do not sufficiently recognize the ecological importance of decadent trees and their derivatives, snags and down boles (Fig. 10). The numerous and important roles of dead wood, both snags and logs, are well known (see e.g., Harmon et al. 2004, Maser et al. 1988). Most individual-tree selection systems involve the systematic removal of decadent, diseased, or poorly formed trees, although some practitioners explicitly retain such trees for ecological purposes, especially as wildlife habitat (Mitchell et al. 2000). Additionally, windthrows generate localized soil disturbance (Fig. 11), which is not emulated with selection systems.

Figure 10.—A snag and downed log left after a small-scale canopy disturbance in an old-growth northern hardwood forest. Photo credit: Steven Katovich, USDA Forest Service, www.forestryimages.org.

Figure 11.—Localized soil disturbance in the form of a tipped-up root wad is characteristic of many tree blowdowns.

Figure 12.—A disturbance gap within a Sierra Nevada mixed conifer forest in Yosemite National Park, California; note the biological legacies of snags and downed boles, as well as natural regeneration of ponderosa pine and associated species within the gap.

Group Selection

Traditional group selection harvest practices contrast in their biological legacies with multi-tree, gap-based natural disturbance regimes. Natural multi-tree gap disturbances leave behind significant biological legacies, including snags or downed boles or both (Fig. 12). Depending upon the disturbance agent, there may be living legacies, such as intact understory layers (including seedling banks) and pits-and-mounds in the case of wind-created gaps. Few silvicultural prescriptions based upon group selection have explicitly incorporated such structural legacies (Table 3).

Contrasts in opening size between multi-tree gap disturbance and traditional group selection also are common. Group selection prescriptions generally use larger (sometimes several times larger) openings on average than the size of gaps created by natural disturbance processes. For example, group selections proposed as the primary harvest method in mixed-conifer types on national forests in the Sierra Nevada involve 1- to 2-ha openings. A "gap" of this size is many times larger than the size of natural gaps (typically 0.08- to 0.10-ha) that are typically found within these forests (e.g., Knight 1997).

Natural gaps generally exhibit a range in sizes typified by a distribution heavily skewed toward smaller openings (e.g., Rebertus et al. 1997). Factors influencing foresters to deviate from this distribution and select larger than natural average opening sizes under group selection prescriptions include concerns about growth rates of reproduction, cost and operational difficulties associated with harvesting in small areas, and generation of greater revenues during an entry.

Heavy Partial Disturbances vs. Two-Cohort Management Systems

Heavy partial disturbances that create stands with two tree cohorts provide a middle ground along the gradient from even-aged to uneven-aged management (Palik et al. 2002). Heavy partial canopy disturbances are characteristic of a wide array of forest types including Acadian mixed conifer forests (Fajvan and Seymour 1993, Seymour and Hunter 1999) and Great Lakes red pine-white pine forests (Heinselman 1981). Such disturbances result in legacies in the form of dead and down trees, live residual canopy trees, patches of understory plant populations, as well as horizontal heterogeneity in stand structure.

Figure 13.—An early 20th century two-cohort stand of eastern white pine and red pine, after heavy partial canopy disturbance on the Chippewa National Forest, Minnesota.

Heavy partial disturbances often result in higher levels of retention than is characteristic of stand-replacement disturbances, but also remove more of the overstory in any one event than is characteristic of individual tree or gap disturbances. Initially the stand will consist of two distinct age cohorts after regeneration is established (Fig. 13).

In the nomenclature of traditional silviculture, a shelterwood with retention (e.g., retention exceeding 20 percent but less than 60 percent) is an analog to heavy partial canopy disturbance (Palik and Zasada 2002, Seymour and Hunter 1999). However, such systems often are implemented in ways that create homogeneity in stand structure, resource availability, and competitive environments, and pay limited attention to retention of biological legacies (Table 3). For instance, large live trees may be retained more for their economic value, rather then their potential to contribute substantially to structural complexity and wildlife habitat.

The same concerns about lack of legacy management in even-aged systems generally are concerns for two-aged systems. Residual trees may be dispersed uniformly across the stand, creating fairly uniform environments for new regeneration. A primary consideration when retaining

overstory trees in such systems has been their expected growth and yield potential and, hence, financial return. There also may be interest in providing adequate seed sources for a new cohort. For both reasons, a single tree species may be selected preferentially for retention. As with selection systems, two-cohort management may not explicitly consider the ecological importance of large decadent trees. Such trees, including dying, diseased, or poorly formed trees, generally are considered liabilities and are removed during harvest operations.

TREE MORTALITY PROCESSES DURING STAND DEVELOPMENT

Various conceptual models have been used to describe the processes and outcomes of stand or patch development following tree-initiating disturbances, particularly large-scale disturbance. These include relatively simple four-stage models that focus largely on live tree cohort establishment and development of vertical patterns (Oliver and Larson 1996) or those based on ecosystem processes, such as biomass accumulation and nutrient cycles (Bormann and Likens 1979). A recent, more complex model of stand development (Franklin et al. 2002) specifically considers the role of tree growth and decline, plant competition and competition-induced mortality, and small-scale disturbances during

Figure 14.—Cross-section of a 650-year-old stand of western red cedar, Douglas-fir, and western hemlock (Cedar Flats Research Natural Area, Washington), illustrating the mosaic of structural patches characteristic of old-growth stands in the Pacific Northwest. This mosaic is the consequence of centuries of development, including small-scale canopy disturbance, within a stand that was initially of even structure and age. Drawing courtesy of Robert Van Pelt.

stand development as generators of complexity and heterogeneity in structure and composition.

Consideration of these developmental processes, particularly those related to tree mortality, and their structural outcomes is essential to the formulation of comprehensive ecological forestry prescriptions that include intermediate silvicultural treatments. The complex structures and spatial heterogeneity that are distinctive features of mature and old-growth forest are often the result of mortality processes occurring during stand development (Fig. 14), i.e., after the stand initiation (sensu Oliver and Larson 1996) or stand disturbance and legacy creation stage (sensu Franklin et al. 2002).

Competitive Tree Mortality

Competitive tree mortality, or natural thinning, results from competition for light and soil resources among trees in a stand or patch (Oliver and Larson 1996). Although often viewed as a continuous process, competitive mortality may occur in pulses over the course of stand development (Horsley et al. 2000, Palik and Pregitzer 1993b). As trees grow in size, they occupy more growing space and compete for limited resources. Many trees in the stand may decline in growth as competition intensifies; however, inferior competitors decline in growth and vigor at a faster rate than superior competitors, and the former eventually die. This mortality frees growing space and resources, which in turn allows growth rates of vigorous trees to increase until the next period of competitive interaction and resultant mortality.

A key feature of competitive exclusion is that trees generally die from below; that is, the smallest, weakest trees die, leaving larger, more vigorous individuals to use liberated resources (Oliver and Larson 1996). The result of this process is the development of larger trees, as well as some size variation within the stand, particularly when multiple tree species of different shade tolerance are present (Nyland 2002). Additional results include the development of associated structural features, such as large branches and extensive heartwood. Competitive tree mortality also generates snags and dead wood on the ground, but this material is typically small and thus of limited value as habitat and a modifier of microclimate (Fig. 15).

Figure 15.—Dead wood generated by competitive tree mortality in a stand in the Cedar River Watershed, King County, Washington. This material is typically small in size and not persistent and consequently has limited habitat value. Photo credit: James A. Lutz.

Figure 16.—A dense patch of longleaf pine regeneration developing within a canopy gap at the Jones Ecological Research Center, Georgia. Competitive tree mortality occurs among trees within this gap.

In forests generated from stand-replacing disturbances, competitive tree mortality continues to occur over time, but is increasingly concentrated in spatially distinct patches as the stand transitions into the maturation phase of development (Franklin et al. 2002). Of course, in forests characterized by tree-scale and gap-scale disturbance, competitive thinning always occurs within discrete patches of trees that have established or been released in large canopy gaps (Fig. 16).

In natural forests, competitive tree mortality does not progress uniformly throughout a stand, due to spatial variation in initial tree density, microenvironment, vigor, and species composition. Consequently, different portions of the stand will thin at different rates and the residual trees will grow at different rates. The result is some small degree of horizontal variation in stand density, tree sizes, and vigor; however, this horizontal variation for the most part develops as a result of noncompetitive tree mortality, as described below.

Noncompetitive Tree Mortality

Competition-induced tree mortality is augmented by small-scale canopy disturbances (Fig. 17). Single tree and small gap mortality can occur throughout the life of a forest stand, although the probability of occurrence increases with stand age, becoming particularly important after the initial period of exponential stand growth and competitive mortality (Franklin et al. 2002). A key element

of this mortality is that it is not directly the result of competition, although trees weakened from competition may be more susceptible to exogenous disturbance.

Agents of small-scale mortality include root rots, wind, bark beetles, lightning, ice damage, and surface fire (Franklin et al. 1987, Franklin and DeBell 1988, Harcombe and Marks 1983, Kneeshaw and Bergeron 1998, Palik and Pederson 1996). Many of these same agents could be part of a stand or patch initiating regeneration disturbance, as described previously. We distinguish small-scale mortality from the latter based on their cumulative spatial influence in the stand; small-scale disturbances may occur infrequently enough and at younger stand ages, such that a significant amount of

Figure 17.—Single-tree canopy disturbance in an old-growth hardwood forest. Toumey Forest, East Lansing, Michigan.

Table 4.—Contrasts between the outcomes of tree mortality processes and traditional thinning treatments

| | Unmanaged stand | | | Managed stand | |
Process	Cause	Outcomes	Treatment	Purpose	Outcomes
Competitive tree mortality	Resource competition	-Larger trees retained -Competitively superior trees favored regardless of species -Shift toward uniform tree size distribution, but variability occurs -Tree quality and form will vary	Silvicultural thinning	-Free growing space for crop trees -Capture economically valuable wood before mortality	-Larger trees favored -Commercial species favored -Strong shift toward uniform tree size distribution -Poor quality trees removed
Small-scale canopy disturbance	Exogenous agents (ice, wind, fire, insects, disease)	-Dominant individuals removed -Creation of canopy openings -Canopy closure from adjacent trees -Height recruitment of existing regeneration -Establishment of regeneration -Establishment or growth of shrub and herbaceous plants -Generation of snags or large wood on the ground	Few silvicultural analogs implemented as an intermediate treatment, as opposed to a regeneration treatment		

regeneration of future overstory trees is not necessarily an outcome. In reality, small-scale mortality events grade into gap-based regeneration disturbances.

Outcomes characteristic of small-scale disturbance include formation of small canopy gaps and generation of large dead wood, including snags and downed boles. Moreover, the opening of small gaps, either above or below the ground, will increase resource availability locally. Neighboring trees may capture these resources and increase growth accordingly (similar to competition-induced mortality), closing the gap laterally (Parsons et al. 1994). Alternatively, gaps may result in new establishment or proliferation of understory plant populations, including herbs, shrubs, and understory trees (McGuire et al. 2001).

Small-scale canopy disturbances are patchy in occurrence across a stand and variable in frequency over time. As a consequence, the development of significant structural heterogeneity, both vertically and horizontally, within a stand is a fundamental outcome of such canopy disturbances. This heterogeneity in canopy conditions results in spatial variability in many stand attributes, including abundances of tree, shrub, and herbaceous plant populations, snag and downed wood loadings, tree size distributions, forest floor conditions, and mineral soil exposure.

COMPARISONS TO TRADITIONAL THINNING TREATMENTS

Contrasts between tree mortality during stand development and traditional applications of silvicultural thinning center on the creation of heterogeneous versus homogeneous structural and compositional stand conditions (Table 4). In a relative sense, natural tree mortality, particularly noncompetitive mortality, generates heterogeneous stand conditions, whereas

Figure 18.—Unthinned (left) and thinned (right) stands of lodgepole pine. Photo credit: USDA Forest Service - Rocky Mountain Region Archives, www.forestryimages.org.

thinning, as traditionally implemented, tends to homogenize the structure and composition of a stand.

Silvicultural thinning, whether pre-commercial or commercial, often has a basic goal of removing trees that are likely to die in the near future, thereby directing resources to and concentrating growth on remaining (crop) trees. In the case of commercial thinning, the harvested trees are of a size to be economically valuable; hence the operation is designed to capture mortality of usable wood before death actually occurs.

Thinning bypasses the process of competitive mortality and, in so doing, can be a valuable tool to facilitate the development of large trees. While competitive mortality as a process does tend to result in more homogeneous distributions of trees than were present before its initiation, silvicultural thinning carries this homogenizing process to the extreme. Thinning is often distributed across a stand specifically to create a uniform distribution of crop trees, efficiently distributing access to resources to those individuals that will eventually be harvested (Fig. 18).

Thinning is also used to improve and standardize tree quality and form (Smith et al. 1996). Poor quality trees, as measured from an economic standpoint— e.g., those with cavities, large branches, or decay pockets—may be preferentially removed (Graves et al. 2000). The long-term goal is to retain only healthy, ostensibly genetically

superior trees. Only recently have the contributions that "non-standard" trees make to biodiversity and wildlife habitat been considered in thinning prescriptions (e.g., Carey 1995) (Fig. 19).

Figure 19.—Sugar maple wildlife tree created by pileated woodpeckers (*Dryocopus pileatus* (L.)) on the Argonne Experimental Forest, Wisconsin. Photo credit: Terry Strong.

The contrasts between small-scale canopy disturbance (non-competitive tree mortality) occurring during stand development and typical thinning practices are significant, largely because the latter typically do not include an analog for small gap-creating disturbances, unless they are specifically part of a gap-based regeneration prescription. Traditionally, timber management specifically seeks to avoid any disturbance-based mortality, especially when it kills dominant trees and tends to be spatially aggregated, i.e., creates canopy gaps. Such mortality has typically not been viewed as a part of natural or, at least, acceptable stand development processes. As a consequence, applications of silvicultural thinning to create structural heterogeneity have been limited.

RECOVERY PERIODS BETWEEN DISTURBANCE EVENTS
Stand-Replacement Disturbance

Stand-initiating natural disturbances vary not only in their type, scale, intensity, and legacies they produce, but also in their frequency. Often, but not always, the return interval between stand-initiating events is long enough that structural complexity, particularly as a result of noncompetitive mortality processes, can develop (Fig. 20). For example, the predicted return interval for Class 4 stand-replacing hurricanes in Coastal Plain pine forests in South Carolina is 260 years (Myers and van Lear 1998). Between these major disturbances, small-scale tree mortality events occur with increasing frequency as stands age (Palik and Pederson 1996), leading to development of complex heterogeneous stand conditions.

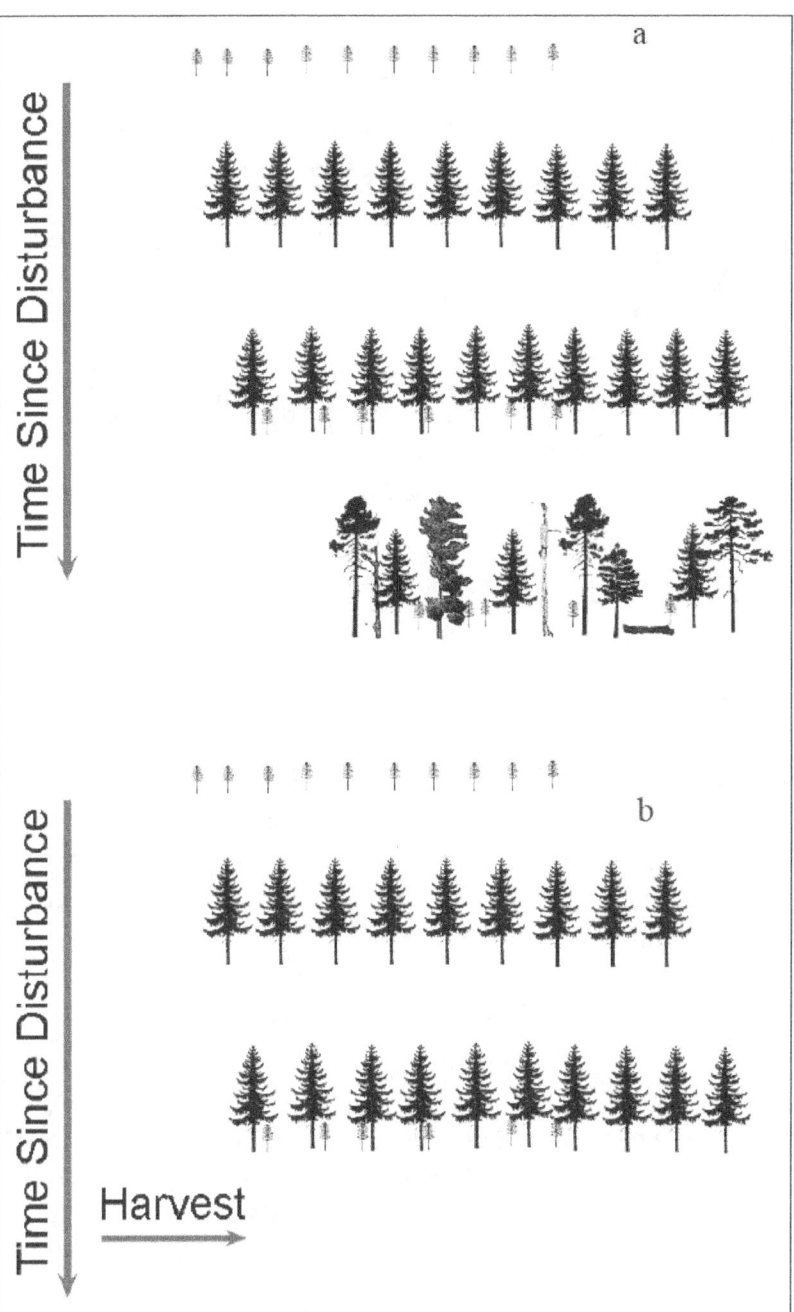

Figure 20.—Conceptual representation of the development of stand-scale ecological complexity. (a) A young post-disturbance stand begins with simplified structure and composition and over time develops significant structural complexity due primarily to small-scale canopy disturbance. (b) In many traditional forestry approaches, the stand is harvested before significant compositional and structural complexity has had time to develop.

The importance of recovery period for development of structural complexity is well illustrated by the dynamics of large dead wood in Pacific Northwest Douglas-fir forests. Spies et al. (1988) illustrate the temporal dynamics of large wood after stand-initiating fires (Fig. 21). They show that initial high loadings of dead wood before disturbance increase dramatically after a fire, primarily due to fire mortality, with lesser contributions

21

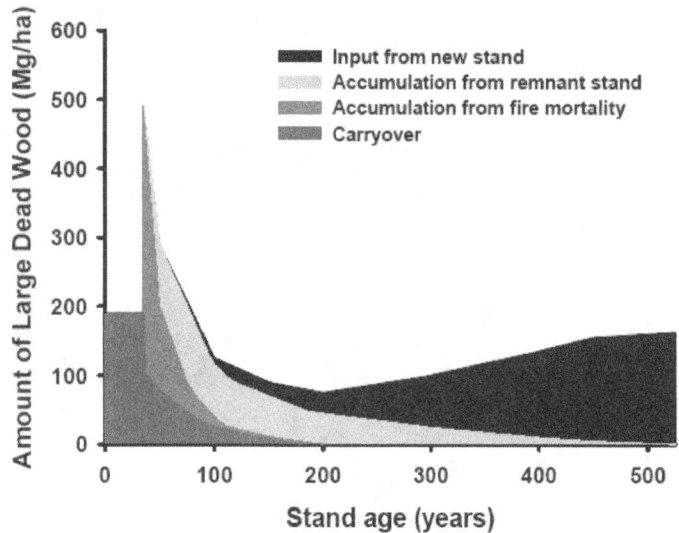

Figure 21.—The development of structural complexity over time as illustrated by the dynamics of large dead wood in Pacific Northwest Douglas-fir dominated forests after partial stand-replacement fire. Dead wood is derived from four sources, including carryover from the pre-disturbance stand, mortality from the fire, mortality from the post-disturbance residual stand, and the newly developing stand. Redrawn from Spies et al. 1988.

from carryover from the previous stand and, in the case of partial burns, contributions from the residual stand after the fire. Wood levels then decline dramatically within the first 150 to 200 years of stand development, falling well below initial post-disturbance values. Several centuries are required before the amount of large, persistent dead wood increases to values approaching pre-disturbance levels, primarily as a result of small-scale canopy disturbances and mortality in the developing stand (Agee 1993, Franklin et al. 2002, Hemstrom and Franklin 1982). While the time period required to develop comparable levels of complexity is probably not as long in most forest types as in Douglas-fir, the general premise still applies; it takes a significant period of time between major disturbances for small-scale mortality processes to create a spatially complex and heterogeneous forest.

Single Tree and Gap Disturbances

The concept of recovery period is clearly applicable to stand-replacement disturbance regimes. However, there is value in considering this concept in the context of gap-replacement regimes as well. Forests that develop primarily as a result of gap-disturbance regimes, e.g., hardwood forest in eastern North America (Frelich and Lorimer 1991, Runkle 1982), are spatially heterogeneous and structurally complex precisely because gaps occur infrequently in space and time, creating a patch mosaic of forest in different stages of development. At the stand

scale, this mosaic of recovering patches includes recent canopy openings in which dead wood is recruited, resource availability is increased, and new cohorts of trees and other plants are established. Although gaps might recur at or near the same location by chance, there often is a long recovery period between gap events at any one location. This allows for the development of large old trees, cavities, and ultimately a source of large snags and dead wood on the ground.

CONTRASTS BETWEEN RECOVERY PERIODS AND ROTATION LENGTH

In commodity-oriented forestry, stands invariably are terminated before significant structural complexity has developed, even though substantial biomass may have accumulated (Fig. 20). Consequently, commercially managed stands typically lack trees of very large diameter, significant amounts of coarse wood, and trees with unique structures (e.g., cavities, large limbs, heartwood, and brooms). Moreover, they often are low in tree species diversity because the time between harvest cycles is insufficient for tolerant species to establish or to advance into intermediate and co-dominant canopy positions in stands. This problem is compounded when stands are deliberately or inadvertently simplified during establishment, e.g., if no legacies are retained or only a single species is planted. An example of this is seen in Great Lakes aspen forests. Most of these forests originated in the early part of the 20th century after widespread

Figure 22.—A regenerating aspen stand in northern Michigan. Except for the older eastern white pine, the stand is devoid of biological legacies from the previous stand and is simplified and homogeneous in structure. Photo credit: Kurt Pregitzer.

logging followed by intense slash fires (Graham et al. 1963). Many managed aspen stands are devoid of any significant biological legacies and are spatially homogeneous (Fig. 22). Moreover, the traditional management prescription calls for clearcut harvesting of stands at 60 to 80 years of age—typically before significant structural and compositional complexity has developed.

The motivation for terminating stands before development of structural complexity is often driven by economic factors. On many timberlands managed for commodities the prevailing practice is to base rotation age on financial calculations, particularly discounted present net value (Davis et al. 2001); long rotations are an anathema using this criterion. Government resource agencies (e.g., USDA Forest Service) use culmination of mean annual growth increment in which rotation age is determined by the growth rate of crop trees. A problem with this approach is that in unthinned stands, time to growth culmination can be quite short, relative to tree lifespans. For instance, volume growth of site index 170 Douglas-fir culminates at around 65 years (as cited in Daniel et al. 1979)—well before much structural complexity has developed in this particularly long-lived forest type.

FORMULATING AN ECOLOGICAL FORESTRY APPROACH

Prescriptions incorporating classical silvicultural systems provide a comprehensive plan for regeneration and tending of forest stands through time. The classic systems encompass all stages of stand development from regeneration to harvest of mature trees (Barrett 1994, Burns 1983, Nyland 2002, Smith et al. 1996). Silvicultural approaches that incorporate an understanding of natural disturbances and stand development processes, i.e., an ecological forestry approach, need to be similarly comprehensive. Although we do not address all components of an ecological forestry prescription, it is our view that at a minimum, relevant management activities for ecological forestry must incorporate an understanding of tree-regenerating disturbance events that create biological legacies, less intense disturbances and mortality that affect the structural development of the established stand, and the importance of recovery periods between disturbance events as a process leading to greater ecological complexity within a stand. In this section, we provide some guiding principles to develop such prescriptions, in the context of the three-legged stool of ecological forestry (Sidebar 1). For examples of comprehensive silvicultural prescriptions that incorporate ecological concepts, we refer the reader to specific case studies (e.g., Beese 1995, Mitchell et al. 2000, Pecore 1992, Seymour et al. 2006).

An essential first step in applying principles from natural disturbance and stand development to ecological forestry is understanding that creating and perpetuating appropriate structural, functional, and compositional attributes is often a primary management goal. "Appropriate" here means attributes that achieve defined goals, which in ecological forestry always include ecological objectives. We are not suggesting that silvicultural systems should be precisely modeled on natural disturbances and stand development processes, because this is not possible (Palik et al. 2002). Rather, the objective is to understand natural processes and resultant patterns and draw upon this understanding to design silvicultural approaches that achieve ecological and other management goals.

Three principles form the basis of an ecological forestry program (in our analogy, the three legs that support the stool of ecological forestry):

1. Incorporating biological legacies into harvest prescriptions

2. Incorporating natural stand development processes, including small-scale disturbance, into intermediate treatments

3. Allowing for appropriate recovery periods between regeneration harvests

We review each of these principles in more detail below.

Principle 1: Incorporating Biological Legacies into Harvest Prescriptions

Incorporating management of biological legacies into regeneration harvest prescriptions is the first fundamental principle of ecological forestry. Referencing our earlier discussion, we know that legacies include important structures from existing stands, such as large healthy trees, decadent trees, snags, and boles, and other coarse woody on the forest floor. Such structures typically 1) persist as legacies even through the most intense stand-replacement disturbances; 2) play critical roles as habitat and modifiers of the physical environment; and 3) are difficult or impossible to re-create once removed from managed stands, hence the need to carry them over from the pre-disturbance stand. Directly and indirectly, such structural legacies lifeboat many elements of biodiversity, whether these elements are explicitly identified or not, and where a stand-replacement disturbance regime prevails, structurally enrich the new stand.

Retention of compositional legacies (e.g., various tree species and other plants) also is an important consideration. For example, retention of certain species is often an explicit element of a retention prescription. Sometimes this will actually be done in order to retain structures or structural conditions of a specific type, such as with retention of a hardwood component in an otherwise conifer-dominated stand. Compositional retention should consider both commercial and noncommercial species; historically, noncommercial species often are removed despite their ecological value.

For instance, non-commercial hardwood species have routinely been removed in Finno-Scandinavian conifer forests, potentially reducing populations of lichens that are unique to these species (Kuusinen 1994). Retention may also be prescribed to maintain species with special functional capabilities, such as nitrogen fixation.

Increasingly, retention of biological legacies, particularly structural legacies, is being incorporated into harvest prescriptions throughout the temperate forest regions of the world (Franklin et al. 1997, Lindenmayer and Franklin 2002, Palik and Zasada 2002, Vanha-Majamaa and Jalonen 2001). This approach has been labeled "variable retention harvesting" (VRH) and is defined as:

"... an approach to harvesting based on the retention of structural elements or biological legacies (trees, snags, logs, etc.) from the harvested stand for integration into the new stand to achieve various ecological objectives... Major variables are types, densities, and spatial arrangements of retained structures" (Helms 1998).

In British Columbia the approach has been formalized legally as the "Variable Retention Harvest System" as follows:

"Retention system means a silvicultural system that is designed to: (a) retain individual trees to maintain the structural diversity over the area of the cut block for at least one rotation; and (b) leave more than half of the total area of the cut block within one tree height from the base of a tree or group of trees, whether or not the tree or group of trees is within the cut block" (Mitchell and Beese 2002).

VRH prescriptions must address three fundamental issues including what to retain, how much to retain, and what the spatial pattern of retention should be—e.g., spatially dispersed or aggregated in the harvest unit. Decisions on these three variables obviously must be related to specific management goals, priorities among goals, and type of silvicultural system used (e.g., stand replacing, two-cohort, or selection); consequently, a broad spectrum of specific prescriptions is possible (Fig. 23) (Franklin et al. 1997, Lindenmayer and Franklin 2002).

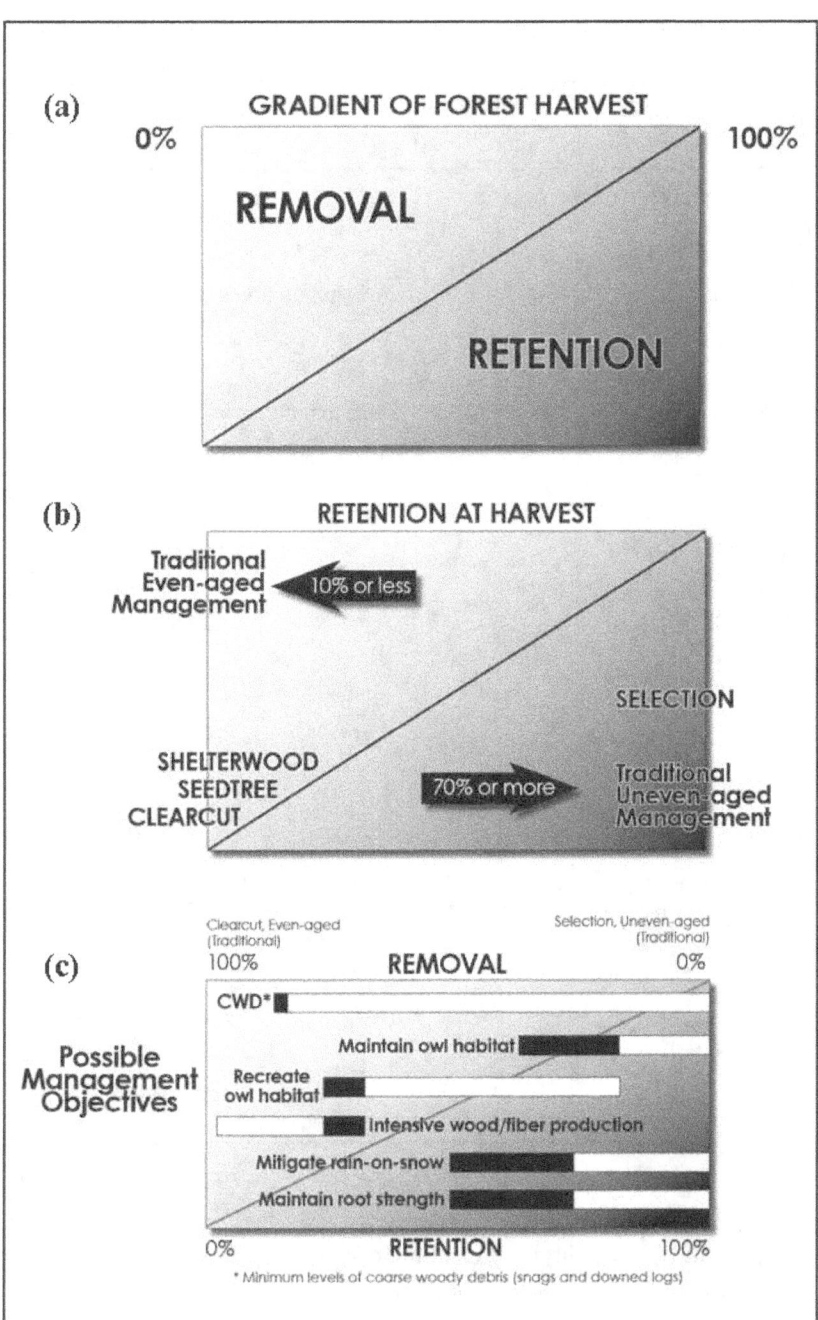

(a)
GRADIENT OF FOREST HARVEST
0%   100%
REMOVAL
RETENTION

(b)
RETENTION AT HARVEST
Traditional Even-aged Management ← 10% or less
SELECTION
SHELTERWOOD SEEDTREE CLEARCUT
70% or more → Traditional Uneven-aged Management

(c)
Clearcut, Even-aged (Traditional)   Selection, Uneven-aged (Traditional)
100%   REMOVAL   0%
Possible Management Objectives
CWD*
Maintain owl habitat
Recreate owl habitat
Intensive wood/fiber production
Mitigate rain-on-snow
Maintain root strength
0%   RETENTION   100%
* Minimum levels of coarse woody debris (snags and downed logs)

Figure 23.—Variable retention harvesting represents a continuum of possibilities; (a) which traditional forest harvest systems have only partially exploited; (b) but which can be exploited to respond to a range of management goals (c).

Incorporating Legacies into Stand-Replacement Systems

Incorporating biological legacies into traditional even-aged harvest practices is the most obvious way to better approximate the outcomes of natural stand-replacing disturbances. In fact, VRH has most often been used to modify traditional even-aged management in forest types and sites characterized by stand-replacement disturbances. Legacies typically selected for retention are large structures--including large old and often decadent trees, snags, and downed boles--that fulfill many important ecological functions (Fig. 24) and often take decades to centuries to develop in new stands.

The spatial pattern of retention in stand-replacement systems is an interesting issue because some ecological objectives are best met by dispersing retained structures and others are best served by concentrating the retention

Table 5.—Hypothesized effects of spatially dispersed and aggregate structural retention on ecosystem characteristics and objectives

Characteristic or objective	Spatial pattern of retention	
	Dispersed	Aggregate
Microclimate modification	Less: generalized over harvest area	More: localized within harvest area
Influence of geohydrological processes	Same as above	Same as above
Maintenance of root strength	Same as above	Same as above
Retention of diverse tree sizes, species, and conditions	Low probability	High probability
Retention of large-diameter trees	More emphasis	Less emphasis
Retention of multiple vegetation layers	Low probability	High probability
Retention of snags	Difficult	Readily accomplished
Retention of areas of minimal forest floor and understory disturbance	Limited possibilities	Yes
Retention of structurally intact forest habitat patches	Not possible	Possible
Distributed sources of coarse woody debris	Yes	No
Distributed sources of arboreal energy to maintain belowground processes	Yes	No
Windthrow hazard of residual trees	Average wind firmness greater (strong dominants), but trees are isolated	Average wind firmness less, but trees have mutual support
Residual tree damage	High probability	Low probability
Tree form and geometry	Uniform	Variable
Distribution of fine fuels	Uniform	Variable
Regeneration growth (intolerant species)	Lower (impacts generalized over harvest area)	Higher (impacts are localized)
Regeneration growth (tolerant species)	Higher	Lower (outcompeted between aggregates)

(Aubry et al. 2004, Franklin et al. 1997) (Table 5). For example, aggregate retention in stand-replacement systems (and in two-cohort systems as described below) is an obvious way to provide some protection from harvest disturbance to understory plants and the forest floor, an important consideration in ecological forestry (Kirkman et al. 2004). Different patterns of retention also may have profoundly different effects on growth and productivity of regenerating trees (Palik et al. 2003, 2005). As the name suggests, one common goal of VRH systems is incorporating spatial heterogeneity of retention within a harvest unit, ranging from dispersed to aggregate within the same harvest unit (Fig. 25).

Modifying clearcut and shelterwood prescriptions to incorporate wildlife trees, snags, and logs is widely practiced today and represents a first step towards more effective legacy management. Even-aged harvesting with "reserves" is a more formalized approach to incorporating some legacies into traditional harvest methods. However, this approach rarely explicitly recognizes the multiple ecological roles played by such "reserved" structures or the nearly infinite array of structural retention prescriptions possible, such as spatially variable patterns of retention.

Confusion or misunderstanding can also arise from use of the term "reserves." When significant structural

Figure 24.—Typical structures retained on a harvest unit on public lands in the Douglas-fir region, Pacific Northwest, include large, decadent live trees, large snags, and large downed boles, all of which are impossible to re-create in stands managed under even moderate (e.g., 100-year) rotations.

Figure 25.—Variable retention harvesting in Oregon. Spatial pattern of retention includes both dispersed and aggregate within the same harvest unit.

Figure 26.—Overstory retention of eastern white pine, with a new cohort of pines developing below it, after partial harvest in a Great Lakes mixed-pine ecosystem, Minnesota. A goal in this stand is to retain a population of large old pines for extended periods for both ecological and economic reasons. Photo credit: Elizabeth Jacqmain.

legacies are retained in an area identified as a clearcut, most observers will be confused because the area is clearly not a clearcut. Using terms like "reserve shelterwood" or "seed tree" is misleading when the primary goal for retaining large trees is sustaining ecological services, rather than regeneration potential.

In marking structures for retention, attention should be given to retaining a diversity of tree species. "Cleaning" stands by eliminating noncommercial species may have significant negative impacts on biological diversity (Palik and Engstrom 1999). Similarly, emphasis should be given to retaining trees across a range of size classes and levels of decadence. Different types of disturbance tend to remove trees predominantly from one end of the size range or the other; for example, wind tends to thin from above while surface fire thins from below. However, most natural disturbances leave trees across a range of sizes (e.g., Elmqvist et al. 2001, Palik and Robl 1999, Peterson 2004), unlike traditional shelterwood and seed tree applications. Retaining trees in various states of decadence is important for providing critical habitat features, such as cavities, and to ensure a sustained source of large dead wood.

Based on these guidelines, an important question when judging the ecological success of retention is whether the retained species and structures (e.g., snags) represent the range of sizes and physical conditions that typically exist in the stand following a natural disturbance. If the answer to this question is no, then the success of the retention harvest from an ecological standpoint may be in doubt. If retained trees consist primarily of the poorly formed, small, and noncommercial elements, then the prescription is certainly inappropriate.

Incorporating Legacies into Two-Cohort Systems
Two-cohort management systems provide excellent opportunities to incorporate concepts of legacy management into silviculture with only minor adjustments (O'Hara 2001). The key adjustment is to incorporate greater heterogeneity in structural and compositional conditions in the post-harvest stand. For example, retention of overstory trees in two-cohort stands can range from relatively dispersed to relative aggregated within the same harvest unit, resulting in a variety of resource and competitive environments (Palik and Zasada 2002).

An important and broadly applicable principle in managing two-cohort stands is to sustain some desired population of large old trees (Fig. 26) and the derivative large snags and large downed boles they provide. This is one goal implicit in most VRH prescriptions, whether

28

in even-, two-, or uneven-aged stands. However, perpetuating a specific tree population obviously goes beyond the immediate goal of lifeboating organisms and processes and makes explicit the need to manage the remainder of the stand to provide for replacement trees.

Incorporating Legacies into Selection Systems

Structural and compositional retention is also relevant to silvicultural prescriptions for multi-cohort stands, i.e., for forest types subject to tree- or gap-based disturbance regimes. Selection silviculture can be modified to incorporate biological legacies at the tree and gap scale, along with stand-level goals that provide for compositional richness and structural complexity characteristic of gap-driven systems. Such an approach maintains the landscape matrix in a mature forest condition, which is one of the most important environmental aspects of uneven-aged forestry. Marking guidelines can explicitly incorporate goals of maintaining old and large trees indefinitely and as a consequence as source for large snags and downed boles. Examples of such approaches are being applied in several regions (Keeton 2005, Mitchell et al. 2000, USDA Forest Service 2004).

Prescriptions based on group selection can and usually should explicitly incorporate retention of trees, snags and downed boles, particularly at larger gap sizes (Fig. 27). Retention within the gaps can be augmented by permanently reserving a certain percentage of the stand from any future harvest, thereby ensuring that some completely intact structural patches will persist indefinitely. Such prescriptions are being applied to such diverse forest types as coast redwood and eastern hardwood forests. Group selection prescriptions in mixed-conifer types on national forests in the Sierra Nevada provide for structural retention by requiring that all trees >30 inches diameter at breast height (d.b.h.) be retained; the intention is to retain these structures in perpetuity (Verner et al. 1992).

Opening sizes and shapes prescribed under group selection should also vary to more closely match the sizes and shapes of gaps created by natural disturbances, rather than using a standard Varying group size to match the variability in opening ized ("cookie cutter") opening.

Figure 27.—Structural retention with a group selection opening on the Chippewa National Forest, Minnesota.

sizes observed in natural stands is likely to result in a distribution skewed towards smaller average opening sizes. Although tree growth rates, particularly of shade-intolerant species, may be less than those achievable in clearcuts, reduced growth rates should not be a key concern when practicing ecological forestry. In many cases, establishment and early survival of regeneration are likely to be much better with partial shade than in the open conditions associated with larger openings, even for species highly intolerant of shade, such as Douglas-fir (e.g., Isaac 1943) and longleaf pine (e.g., McGuire et al. 2001).

Incorporating variable structural objectives within individual stands should be considered for individual tree and small group selection systems (Mitchell et al. 2000). As an example, silvicultural systems that create (if not already present) and maintain a population of large old trees is appropriate for many forest types subject to gap- or tree-based disturbance regimes. North American mixed conifer forests characterized by low severity fire regimes are an example. Large old trees and their derivative structures (large snags and downed boles) were constant and important structural elements of such forests (Covington and Moore 1994, Noel et al. 1998). A management goal in many such forests is to restore and maintain a target population of large old trees, but without requiring that this goal be met on every hectare (e.g., Johnson et al. 2003).

Principle 2: Intermediate Treatments that Enhance Heterogeneity

Managing established stands to sustain or restore structural and compositional heterogeneity is the second important principle of ecological forestry. The primary way this is accomplished is through innovative uses of thinning. For an ecological forestry approach, the goal of thinning is to create structural and compositional heterogeneity throughout the stand, rather than to concentrate growth on selected trees and create spatially uniform stands, as in a traditional forestry approach.

As discussed previously, thinning treatments are generally modeled on natural decline and mortality of trees during stand development. Our focus here is on thinning treatments that are carried out in ways that create and maintain structural and compositional complexity and heterogeneity including:

- Thinning to stimulate development of larger trees
- Variable density thinning to stimulate development of horizontal heterogeneity
- Small gap creation to develop vertical and horizontal heterogeneity and opportunities for establishing and releasing regeneration and other understory components

Standard silvicultural thinning is intended to anticipate natural competition-induced mortality by removing suppressed trees before they die from resource limitations (thinning from below). An important consequence of such thinning is the release of growing space and resources for the remaining trees. Appropriately implemented thinning from below accelerates the development of large-diameter and high-quality trees at rates faster than would occur naturally. The ecological benefits of large trees is reflected in their use as habitat for nesting, roosting, and avoidance of predators, their influence on microenvironment, and their contribution of food resources and fine fuels. Moreover, large trees are important for their derivatives, large snags, wood on the ground, tip-up mounds, and root wads.

There are some fundamental differences in the way thinning is implemented for ecological versus economic goals, even though they have some comparable objectives, such as creation of large diameter trees. Standard silvicultural thinning is intended to create an evenly distributed population of crop trees, all having similar access to light, water, and soil nutrients. In contrast, natural stands undergoing competitive thinning often display some spatial variation in tree densities, growth rates, and tree sizes.

As discussed previously, competitive-based mortality is augmented by small-scale canopy disturbances, from wind, lightning, insects, or fire. Small-scale disturbances are a fundamental feature of natural stand development and contribute greatly to the development of spatial heterogeneity in stand structure (Franklin et al. 2002). We argue that appropriate silvicultural analogs should specifically plan for thinning treatments that replicate the small-scale disturbance or gap-forming processes, along with competition-based mortality.

Within-stand variation in competitive tree mortality, as well as incorporation of small-scale canopy disturbance as an intermediate treatment, can be accomplished simultaneously using an approach known as variable density thinning of VDT (Sidebar 5, Fig. 28). VDT approaches emulate the natural variation that results from small-scale canopy disturbances and competition-based mortality (Carey 2001). VDT prescriptions provide for unthinned areas (sometimes referred to as "skips") and heavily thinned patches ("gaps"), along with intermediate levels of thinning and residual density through the bulk of the stand (Franklin and Lindenmayer 2002, Harrington et al. 2005). The result is much greater spatial variability in stand densities and, consequently, greater structural complexity and heterogeneity of structure (Fig. 29). Ecological benefits of VDT include development of large trees, opportunities for release or new establishment of woody and herbaceous species, and creation of spatially variable microclimatic and habitat conditions.

Sidebar 5.—Variable Density Thinning (VDT)

In practice VDT is implemented by envisioning a grid pattern in the stand that is to be thinned (Harrington et al. 2005). It may be useful to actually lay out a grid on the ground (Fig. 28). Thinning treatments are assigned to each cell, including gaps (removal of all or most trees), skips (no thinning), and thinned. Grid cell size should be defined by characteristics of the forest type (e.g., sizes of small canopy gaps) and objectives. In applications, cell sizes of 0.04 to 0.10 ha for gaps and 0.10 to 0.30 ha for skips have been used, with 10 to 20 percent of cells assigned to gaps, 10 to 20 percent assigned to skips, and the remainder assigned to some level of standard thinning, which can also incorporate variability in resultant density from cell to cell.

When assigning cells to gaps or skips, the practitioner should look for opportunities to tie cell treatments to existing features of the stand. For instance, gap cells might be placed in areas that already have a natural opening or advanced regeneration of a desired species. Similarly, skip cells might be assigned to protect sensitive features, such as a large snag, small wetland, or patch of understory vegetation. When selecting cell size and the distribution of treatments, it is important to remember that the goal of VDT is creation of distinctly heterogeneous conditions across the stand. Very small cell sizes may not result in distinctly different resource and habitat conditions across the stand; similarly, large cell sizes can result in gaps that approach the size of small clearcuts within the stand.

-0.10 ha grid scale

-Vary thinning by 0.10 ha units

-20% skips (black)

-20% gaps (light gray)

-60% thinned (gray)

Figure 28.—Grid approach for implementing variable density thinning.

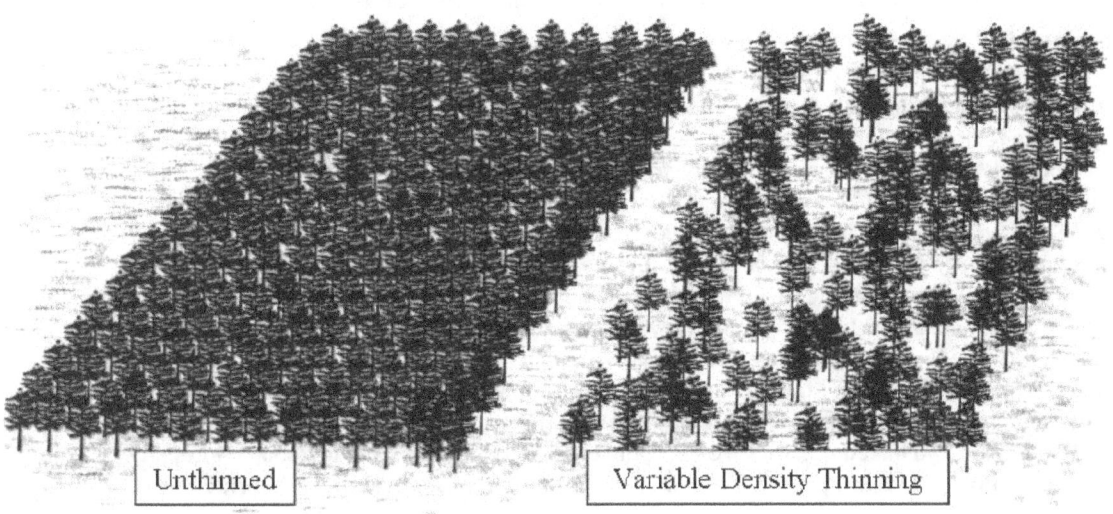

Unthinned

Variable Density Thinning

Figure 29.—Stylized representation of variable density thinning: (a) unthinned stand; (b) thinned stand displaying horizontal variation in stand density including gaps, skips (unthinned areas), and lightly thinned matrix.

Sidebar 6.—Intermediate Treatments that Enhance Structural Heterogeneity of a Stand

Thinning is perhaps the most important intermediate treatment that can be used to enhance structural complexity and heterogeneity in developing stands. However, some additional treatments or approaches can also be used to pursue this objective. Although discussing these activities in detail is beyond the scope of this report, we mention several below.

Decadence creation

This technique involves deliberate killing of living trees or injuring them to induce decline, with the goal of creating dead wood in the form of snags or logs on the ground. Felling trees and girdling trees are examples of techniques used to accomplish this. A more creative approach in systems prone to lightning strikes involves injuring trees in a way that induces a decline and ultimately death, analogous to what might happen after a lighting strike. One technique used to do this involves placing explosive charges within the crown of the tree above the lowest live branches. The resultant explosion will remove most, but not all, of the live crown, followed by death of the tree over one or more years (Fig. 30).

Underplanting

Successional processes in developing stands often involve the establishment of more shade-tolerant tree species from local or introduced seed. When such seed sources are lacking due to past management activities, it may be of interest to underplant the appropriate species with the goal of reintroducing the missing compositional element in the stand. For example, eastern white pine might be underplanted in Great Lakes aspen forests, where past management or disturbances have removed most local seed sources.

Figure 30.—A red pine snag created by removing most of the crown through use of small explosive charges, Chippewa National Forest, Minnesota. Photo credit: Harvey Tjader.

Underplanting might be coordinated with variable density thinning, targeting mid-tolerant species in gaps and more tolerant species in lightly thinned or unthinned portions of the stand.

Prescribed fire

Prescribed surface fire is an underused intermediate treatment in many fire-dependent forest types and one that lends itself to goals of sustaining or restoring understory heterogeneity. Natural surface fires are inherently variable, both in the pattern and size of unburned patches within a burned mosaic, and in the intensity and energy released in the flaming front. As such, surface fires can be used to enhance spatial heterogeneity of understory conditions in burned stands. This variability is in turn a strong driver of high plant diversity that is often a characteristic of fire-dependent ecosystems. Longleaf pine forests of the Southeastern U.S. are well known for this relationship. These systems begin to lose plant diversity on the most productive sites when the burn interval increases beyond once every 3 years and on the less productive sites when the burn interval extends longer than once every 5 years. Frequent surface fire is also important for maintaining characteristic stand structures and reducing catastrophic fire risk in systems dependent on regular burning. For instance, without sufficient burning frequency, fire regimes in ponderosa pine and mixed conifer forests of the Western U.S. shift from low/mixed intensity fires to crown fires, due to dense regeneration providing ladder fuels to connect surface fires to canopy fuels.

Many other intermediate treatments can be used to enhance stand-scale complexity and heterogeneity (Lindenmayer and Franklin 2002). Discussing these in detail is beyond the scope of this report. However, several of these approaches, including decadence creation, underplanting, and prescribed fire, deserve consideration (Sidebar 6, Fig. 30).

Principle 3: Allowing for Appropriate Recovery Periods

The third principle of ecological forestry is to allow for appropriate recovery periods between management entries, especially regeneration harvests (in which case the recovery period is traditionally known as the rotation), to allow complexity to develop (Fig. 20). In ecological forestry, rate of development of desired structures or structural conditions largely determines the length of the recovery period, although these goals do have to be integrated with social and economic objectives. Moreover, it may be desirable to use silvicultural treatments during stand development, such as variable density thinning, to increase the rate at which desired structural features develop (e.g., Carey 2001, Tappeiner et al. 1997).

The principle of allowing appropriate ecological recovery periods between regeneration harvests is potentially a contentious issue because these periods will almost always be much longer than rotations based on economic factors and probably longer than rotations based on growth factors, such as culmination of annual increment. However, culmination of growth increment can be delayed for extended periods of time, through periodic thinning (Curtis 1995, Williamson 1982). This suggests that ecological objectives linked to large old trees can be achieved alongside economic objectives, if the latter involve development of large-diameter, high-quality logs. For example, the mean annual volume increment curve for a 140-year-old red pine stand in northern Minnesota shows extended periods of continued growth, due to periodic growth increases after repeated thinnings which began at age 85 (Fig. 31). In this stand, the quality and value of wood for sawtimber, large poles, and cabin logs continue to increase, as does the ecological significance associated with growing large old red pines.

In short, for ecological forestry, there is little reason to set a rotation age of a stand based solely on financial or growth factors. Rather, the primary determination of harvest age should be the development of acceptable levels of structural complexity, compositional diversity, and within-stand heterogeneity.

ECOLOGICAL FORESTRY: HOW CLOSE TO A NATURAL MODEL?

Mimicking natural disturbance regimes and stand development processes with silviculture is a challenge, if for no other reason than the conditions created by natural processes can never be fully achieved in forests that are also managed for wood production (Palik et al. 2002). However, failure to precisely duplicate these conditions is not a shortfall of the approach but, rather, a consequence of the desire to achieve multiple objectives, i.e., to maintain ecological values and produce some wood for extraction.

The challenge then is to develop approaches that lead to maintenance (or restoration) of ecological complexity, along with opportunities to meet certain timber management goals. The balance may shift toward one goal or the other at different times and different

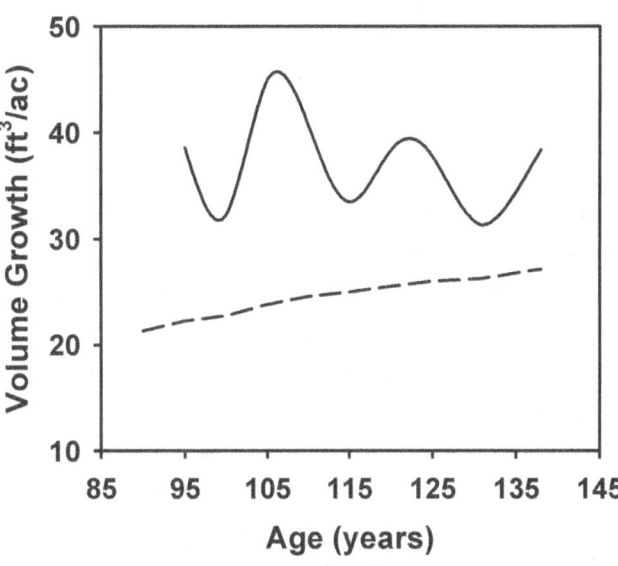

Figure 31.—Volume increment curves for red pine in the Cutfoot Experimental Forest, Minnesota. The forest was thinned seven times, to a growing-stock basal area of 60 ft²/ac beginning at a stand age of 85 years. The dashed line is mean annual increment; the solid line is periodic annual increment (B. Palik, unpublished data).

33

locations, depending upon priorities among management objectives. In many cases, the ultimate objective is to facilitate implementation of silviculture based upon natural disturbance and stand development models without completely ignoring economic objectives. If the latter is ignored, then the former will never be widely implemented at scales needed to achieve significant change in the landscape.

A useful framework for assessing how well the goals of ecological forestry are being met in stands managed for wood production is to quantify discrepancies in complexity between these stands and reference conditions (Sidebar 7, Fig. 32). While the nature of the reference condition is debated (Hunter 1996), and trying to define it is beyond the scope of our discussion, it is important to recognize that for any specific forest type the reference condition actually consists of a domain of conditions that are naturally variable, i.e., a natural range of variation (Landres et al. 1999). As such, reference targets best represent ranges, rather then central tendencies. Moreover, the reference condition includes not only old-growth stands, but also those in various stages of post-disturbance recovery, including very young stands, which typically display high levels of structural and compositional complexity, even after a stand-replacing disturbance (Franklin et al. 1997). Thus, comparisons of managed stands to reference conditions should be made at all stages of development.

When making these comparisons, managers should determine how similar to the reference condition a stand needs to be to achieve ecological forestry goals. The answer is driven by objectives. When managing ecological reserves, the goal probably will be to get as close to the reference condition as possible. When managing for maximum fiber yield, reducing the disparity with the reference condition perhaps is not a consideration. When managing for outcomes within the bulk of the forest landscape, reducing the disparity to the reference condition is likely an important consideration, but in many instances it will be done within the real-world constraints of managing for wood production. In this case, the objective is to devise innovative ways to incorporate the three-legged stool of ecological forestry

into silvicultural prescriptions, while still maintaining some level of timber production as another objective.

Simberloff (1999) suggests that any proposed silvicultural system designed to maintain biodiversity and produce timber should be treated as a hypothesis, due to the limited number of empirical studies to support or refute the approach. The comparative framework we outline can be used to pose such hypotheses and then design silvicultural experiments to test them. For instance, one might hypothesize that as managed systems move closer to the reference condition, productivity of bole wood declines linearly, exponentially, or not at all. Alternatively, one could test the hypothesis that the amount of complexity in managed stands can be increased while maintaining a fixed level of wood production.

The challenge many foresters and forest management organizations now face is the need to develop silvicultural systems that result in stand conditions that incorporate ecological complexity and heterogeneity in much greater degrees than have been considered before (i.e., moving stands closer to reference conditions). Moreover, there is a need to implement these systems on large portions of the forest landscape, i.e., most of the forest where managing for ecological objectives along with wood production is a driving concern. We have intended to facilitate both development and implementation of such systems by providing an overview of the scientific underpinnings of ecological forestry and by synthesizing these underpinnings into generally applicable principles, i.e., the three-legged stool of ecological forestry. Our intent is not to provide a cookbook for developing such systems nor to provide comprehensive silvicultural prescriptions. This is an impossible task given the diversity of ecosystems, objectives, and conditions that must be considered. Moreover, an attempt to do so would be contrary to the creative intent of silviculture as a discipline. Rather, we hope that by distilling key concepts into practical guidelines we can facilitate the development of practices that are adaptable to meet the varied needs and conditions in a wide array of forest ecosystems.

Sidebar 7.—Practical Considerations for Ecological Forestry: How Close to a Reference Condition?

A useful framework for addressing ecological forestry in stands managed for wood is a conceptual model that arrays stands along gradients of (1) management objectives, ranging from production forestry to reserve management, with ecological or matrix management between these endpoints; (2) time or age since disturbance; and (3) variability in degrees of complexity among stands (Fig. 32). In this model, the area in gray represents the domain of natural variability in reference conditions for the system in question, as defined by combinations of time since disturbance and degree of structural and compositional complexity. In other words, this domain represents the array of possible reference conditions for stands in that system; some of which are naturally more complex and some of which are naturally less complex (relative to each other). The dashed rectangles are domains of variability in complexity for management scenarios that differ in the degree to which they achieve multiple objectives of sustaining ecological complexity and wood productivity. Domain A might represent a plantation of an exotic species managed intensively for fiber; note that the range of variability in complexity is not only narrow but also lies outside the range of natural variability. Domain B might include systems managed for large-diameter saw logs and structural complexity, perhaps using two-cohort stands. Notice that the range of variability is narrow relative to the reference condition, but still within the domain of natural variability. Domain C might represent a system managed for maximum similarity to a reference condition, using limited harvesting of lightning- or wind-killed trees, for instance.

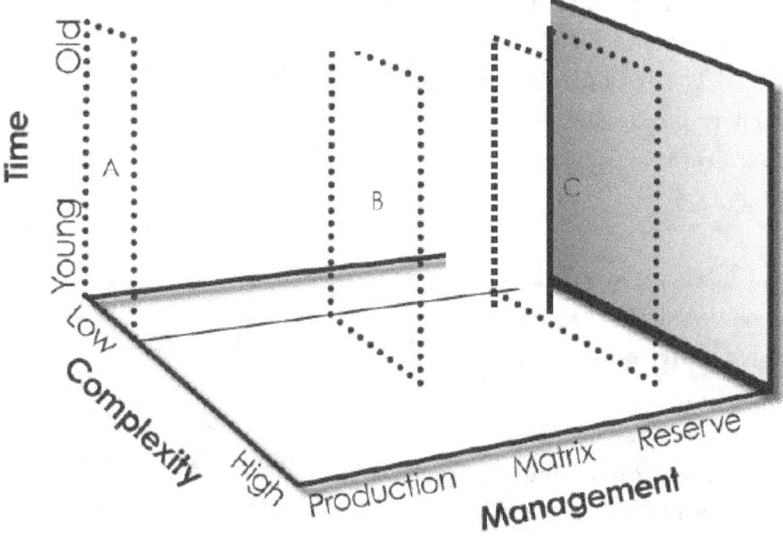

Figure 32.—Three-dimensional conceptual model for judging disparity in ecological complexity between managed forests and reference conditions.

ACKNOWLEDGMENTS

Funding for this project was generously provided by the National Council for Science and Sustainable Forestry. Support also came from the USDA Forest Service Northern Research Station, the Robert Woodruff Foundation, the USDA Forest Service Pacific Northwest Research Station, and McIntyre-Stennis funding.

LITERATURE CITED

Abrams, M.D. 1984. **Uneven-aged jack pine in Michigan.** Journal of Forestry. 82: 306-309.

Adams, D.M.; Ek, A.R. 1974. **Optimizing the management of uneven-aged forest stands.** Canadian Journal of Forest Research. 4: 274-287.

Agee, J.K. 1993. **Fire ecology of Pacific Northwest forests.** Washington, DC: Island Press. 499 p.

Allen, D.A.; Savage, M.; Falk, D.A.; Suckling, K.F.; Swetnam, T.W.; Schulke, T.; Stacey, P.B.; Morgan, P.; Hoffman, M.; Klingel. J.T. 2002. **Ecological restoration of southwestern ponderosa pine ecosystems: a broad perspective.** Ecological Applications. 12: 1418-1433.

Arroyo, M.T.K.; Donoso, C.; Murua, R.F.; Pisano, E.E.; Schlatter, R.P.; Serey, I.A. 1996. **Toward an ecologically sustainable forestry project: concepts, analysis, and recommendations. Protecting biodiversity and ecosystem processes in the Rio Condor Project, tierra del Fuego.** Santiago, Chile: Departamento de Investigacion y Desarollo, Universidad de Chile. 250 p.

Aubry, K.B.; Halpern, C.B.; Maguire, D.A. 2004. **Ecological effects of variable retention harvests in the northwestern United States: the DEMO study.** Forest, Snow, and Landscape Research. 78: 119-137.

Bare, B.B.; Opalach, D. 1988. **Determining investment-efficient diameter distributions for uneven-aged northern hardwoods.** Forest Science. 34: 243-249.

Barrett, J.W., ed. 1994. **Regional silviculture of the United States, 3^d ed.** New York: Wiley. 656 p.

Beese, W.J. 1995. **Montane Alternative Silviculture Systems(MASS): Introduction and objectives.** In: Arnott, J.T.: Beese, W.J.; Mitchell. A.K.; Peterson, J., eds. FRDA Rep. 238. Proceedings of the Montane Alternative Silviculture Systems (MASS) Workshop Canadian Forest Service and British Columbia Ministry of Forestry: 3-8.

Bergeron, Y.; Harvey, B.; Leduc, A.; Gauthier, S. 1999. **Forest management guidelines based on natural disturbance dynamics: stand- and forest-level considerations.** Forestry Chronicle. 75: 49-54.

Bergeron, Y.; Leduc, A.; Harvey, B.D.; Gauthier, S. 2002. **Natural fire regime: a guide for sustainable management of the Canadian boreal forest.** Silva Fennica. 36: 81-95.

Bormann, F.H.; Likens, G.E. 1979. **Pattern and process in a forested ecosystem.** New York: Springer-Verlag. 253 p.

Burns, R.M., ed. 1983. **Silviculture systems for the major forest types of the United States.** Agric. Handb. 445. Washington, DC: U.S. Department of Agriculture, Forest Service. 191 p.

Canham, C.D.; Loucks, O.L. 1984. **Catastrophic windthrow in the presettlement forests of Wisconsin.** Ecology. 65: 803-809.

Carey, A.B. 1995. **Sciurids in Pacific Northwest managed and old-growth forests.** Ecological Applications. 5: 648-661.

Carey, A.B. 2001. **Experimental manipulation of spatial heterogeneity in Douglas-fir forests: effects on squirrels.** Forest Ecology and Management. 152: 13-30.

Christensen, N.L.; Agee, J.K.; Brusssard, P.F.; Hughes, J.; Knight, D.H.; Minshall, G.W.; Peek, J. M.;

Pyne, S.J.; Swanson, F.W.; Thomas, J.W.; Wells, S.; Williams, S.E.; Wright, H.A. 1989. **Interpreting the Yellowstone fires of 1988.** BioScience. 39: 678-685.

Clements, F.E. 1916. **Plant succession: an analysis of the development of vegetation.** Publ. No. 242. Washington, DC: Carnegie Institution of Washington. 1024 p.

Cogbill, C.V. 1996. **Black growth and fiddlebutts: the nature of old-growth red spruce.** In: Davis, M.B., ed. Eastern old-growth forests: prospects for rediscovery and recovery. Washington, DC: Island Press: 113-125.

Covington, W.W.; Moore, M.M. 1994. **Southwestern ponderosa forest structure: changes since Euro-American settlement.** Journal of Forestry. 92: 39-47.

Curtis, J. T. 1959. **The vegetation of Wisconsin.** Madison, WI: University of Wisconsin Press. 657 p.

Curtis, R.O. 1995. **Extended rotations and culmination age of coastal Douglas-fir: old studies speak to current issues.** Res. Pap. PNW-485. Portland, OR: U.S. Department of Agriculture, Forest Service, Pacific Northwest Research Station. 49 p.

Dale, V.H.; Swanson, F.J.; Crisafulli, C.M., eds. 2005. **Ecological responses to the 1980 eruption of Mount St. Helens.** New York: Springer. 347 p.

Daniel, T.W.; Helms, J.A.; Baker, F.S. 1979. **Principles of silviculture.** New York: McGraw-Hill. 500 p.

Davis, L.S.; Johnson, K.N.; Bettinger, P.S.; Howard, T.E. 2001. **Forest management to sustain ecological, economic, and social values. 4ᵗʰ ed.** New York: McGraw. 804 p.

Delong, S.C.; Kessler, W.B. 2000. **Ecological characteristics of mature forest remnants left by wildfire.** Forest Ecology and Management. 131: 93-106.

Eberhart, K.E.; Woodard, P.M. 1987. **Distribution of residual vegetation associated with large fires in Alberta.** Canadian Journal of Forest Research. 117: 1207-1212.

Elmqvist, T.; Wall, M.; Berggren, A.L.; Blix, L.; Fritioff, A.; Rinman, U. 2001. **Tropical forest reorganization after cyclone and fire disturbance in Samoa: remnant trees as biological legacies.** Conservation Ecology 5 [online] URL: http://www.consecol.org/vol5/iss2/art10/.

Erickson, M.D.; Reed, D.D.; Mroz, G.D. 1990. **Stand development and economic analysis of alternative cutting methods in northern hardwoods: 32-year results.** Northern Journal of Applied Forestry. 7: 153-158.

Fajvan, M.A.; Seymour, R.S. 1993. **Canopy stratification, age structure, and development of multicohort stands of eastern white pine, eastern hemlock, and red spruce.** Canadian Journal of Forest Research. 23: 1799-1809.

Foster, D.R.; Aber, J.D.; Melillo, J.M.; Bowden, R.; Bazzaz, F. 1997. **Forest response to disturbance and anthropogenic stress: rethinking the 1938 hurricane and the impact of physical disturbance vs chemical and climate stress on forest ecosystems.** BioScience. 47: 437-445.

Foster, D.R.; Boose, E.R. 1992. **Patterns of forest damage resulting from catastrophic wind in central New England, USA.** Journal of Ecology. 80: 79-98.

Foster, D.R.; Knight, D.H.; Franklin, J.F. 1998. **Landscape patterns and legacies resulting from large, infrequent forest disturbances.** Ecosystems. 1: 497-510.

Franklin, J.F.; Dyrness, C.T. 1973. **Natural vegetation of Oregon and Washington.** Gen. Tech. Rep. PNW-8. Portland, OR: U.S. Department of Agriculture, Forest Service, Pacific Northwest Research Station. 427 p.

Franklin, J.F.; DeBell, D.S. 1988. **Thirty-six years of tree population change in an old-growth *Pseudotsuga-Tsuga* forest.** Canadian Journal of Forest Research. 18: 633-639.

Franklin, J.F.; MacMahon, J.A. 2000. **Messages from a mountain.** Science. 288: 1183-1185.

Franklin, J.F.; Lindenmayer, D.B. 2002. **Conserving forest biodiversity: a comprehensive multiscaled approach.** Washington, DC: Island Press. 352 p.

Franklin, J.F.; Van Pelt, R. 2004. **Spatial aspects of structural complexity in old-growth forests.** Journal of Forestry. 102: 22-28.

Franklin, J.F.; Shugart, H.H.; Harmon, M.E. 1987. **Tree death as an ecological process.** BioScience. 37: 550-556.

Franklin, J.F.; Berg, D.R.; Thornburgh, D.A.; Tappeiner, J.C. 1997. **Alternative silvicultural approaches to timber harvesting: variable retention harvest systems.** In: Kohm, K.A.; Franklin, J.F., eds. Creating a forestry for the 21st century. Washington, DC: Island Press: 111-139.

Franklin, J.F.; Lindenmayer, D.B.; MacMahon, J.A.; McKee, A.; Magnusson, J.; Perry, D.A.; Waide, R.; Foster, D.R. 2000. **Threads of continuity: ecosystem disturbances, biological legacies and ecosystem recovery.** Conservation Biology in Practice. 1: 8-16.

Franklin, J.F.; Spies, T.A.; Van Pelt, R.; Carey, A.B.; Thornburgh, D.A.; Berg, D.R.; Lindenmayer, D.B.; Harmon, M.E.; Keeton, W.S.; Shaw, D.C.; Bible, K.; Chen, J. 2002. **Disturbances and structural development of natural forest ecosystems with silvicultural implications, using Douglas-fir forests as an example.** Forest Ecology and Management. 155: 399-423.

Frelich, L.E.; Lorimer, C.G. 1991. **Natural disturbance regimes in hemlock-hardwood forests of the upper Great Lakes region.** Ecology. 61: 145-164.

Frelich, L.E.; Reich, P.B. 1995. **Spatial patterns and succession in a Minnesota southern-boreal forest.** Ecological Monographs. 65: 325-346.

Galipeau, C.; Kneeshaw, D.D.; Bergeron, Y. 1997. **White spruce and balsam fir colonization of a site in the southeastern boreal forest as observed 68 years after fire.** Canadian Journal of Forest Research. 27: 139-147.

Goff, F.G.; West, D. 1975. **Canopy-understory interaction effects on forest population structure.** Forest Science. 21: 98-108.

Goodburn, J.M.; Lorimer, C.G. 1999. **Population structure in old-growth and managed northern hardwoods: an examination of the balanced diameter distribution concept.** Forest Ecology and Management. 118: 11-29.

Graham, S A.; Harrison, R.P., Jr.; Westell, E.E., Jr. 1963. **Aspens: phoenix trees of the Great Lakes region.** Ann Arbor, MI: University of Michigan Press. 272 p.

Graves, A.T.; Fajvan, M.A.; Miller, G.W. 2000. **The effects of thinning intensity on snag and cavity tree abundance in an Appalachian hardwood stand.** Canadian Journal of Forest Research. 30: 1214-1220.

Gray, A.N.; Spies, T.A. 1996. **Gap size, within-gap position and canopy structure effects on conifer seedling establishment.** Journal of Ecology. 84: 635-646.

Hann, S.W.; Bare, B.B. 1979. **Uneven-aged forest management: state of the art (or science?).** Gen. Tech. Rep. INT-50. Ogden, UT: U.S. Department of Agriculture, Forest Service, Intermountain Research Station. 46 p.

Harcombe, P.A.; Marks, P.L. 1983. **Five years of tree death in a *Fagus-Magnolia* forest, southeast Texas (USA).** Oecologia. 57: 49-54.

Harmon, M.J.; Franklin, J F.; Swanson, F.; Sollins, P.; Gregory, S.V.; Lattin, J.D.; Anderson, N.H.; Cline, S. P.; Aumen, N.G.; Sedell, J.R.; Lienkaemper, G.W.;

Cromack, K.; Cummins. K.W. 2004. **Ecology of coarse woody debris in temperate ecosystems.** Advances in Ecological Research. 34: 59-234.

Harrington, C.A.; Roberts, S.D.; Brodie, L.C. 2005. **Tree and understory responses to variable-density thinning in western Washington.** Gen. Tech. Rep. PNW-635. In: Peterson, C.E.; Maguire, D.A., eds. Balancing ecosystem values: innovative experiments for sustainable forestry. Portland, OR: U.S. Department of Agriculture, Forest Service, Pacific Northwest Research Station: 97-106.

Heinselman, M.L. 1973. **Fire in the virgin forests of the Boundary Waters Canoe Area, Minnesota.** Quaternary Research. 3: 329-382.

Heinselman, M.L. 1981. **Fire intensity and frequency as factors in the distribution and structure of northern ecosystems.** Gen. Tech. Rep. WO-26. In: Proceedings of fire regimes and ecosystem properties. Washington, DC: U.S. Department of Agriculture, Forest Service: 7-57.

Helms, J.A. 1998. **Dictionary of forestry.** Cambridge, MA: Society of American Foresters and CABI Publishing. 210 p.

Hemstrom, M.A.; Franklin, J.F. 1982. **Fire and other disturbances of the forests of Mount Rainier National Park.** Quaternary Research. 18: 32-51.

Hollings, C.S. 1992. **The role of forest insects in structuring the boreal landscape.** In: Shugart, H.H.; Leemans, R.; Bonan, G.B., eds. A systems analysis of the global boreal forested. New York: Cambridge University Press: 170-195.

Horsley, S.B.; Long, R.P.; Bailey, S.W.; Hallett, R.A.; Hall, T.J. 2000. **Factors associated with the decline and disease of sugar maple on the Allegheny Plateau.** Canadian Journal of Forest Research. 30: 1365-1378.

Hunter, M.L., Jr. 1996. **Benchmarks for managing ecosystems: are human activities natural?** Conservation Biology. 10: 695-697.

Hunter, M.L., Jr. 1999. **Maintaining biodiversity in forest ecosystems.** New York: Cambridge University Press. 698 p.

Isaac, L.A. 1943. **Reproductive habits of Douglas-fir.** Washington, DC: Charles Lathrop Pack Foundation. 46 p.

Isaac, L.A.; Meagher, G.S. 1936. **Natural reproduction on the Tillamook Burn two years after the fire.** Portland, OR: U.S. Department of Agriculture, Forest Service, Pacific Northwest Forest and Range Experiment Station. 15 p.

Jacqmain, E.I.; Jones, R.H.; Mitchell, R. J. 1999. **Influences of frequent cool-season burning across a soil moisture gradient on oak community structure in longleaf pine ecosystems.** American Midland Naturalist. 141: 85-100.

James, F.C.; Richards, P.M.; Hess, C.A.; McCluney, K.E.; Walters, E.L.; Schrader, M.S. 2004. **Sustainable forestry for the red-cockaded woodpecker's ecosystem.** In: Costa, R.; Daniels, S.J., eds. Red-cockaded woodpecker: road to recovery. Blaine, WA: Hancock House: 60-69.

Johnson, K.N.; Franklin, J.F.; Johnson, D.L. 2003. **A plan for the Klamath Tribe's management of the Klamath Reservation forest.** Rep. 184. Corvallis, OR: Oregon State University. 120 p.

Kaya, J.; Buongiorno, J. 1989. **A harvesting guide for uneven-aged northern hardwood stands.** Northern Journal of Applied Forestry. 6: 9-14.

Keeton, W. S. 2005. **Managing for old-growth structure in northern hardwood forests.** In: Peterson, C.E.; Maguire, D.A., eds. Balancing ecosystem values: innovative experiments for sustainable forestry. Gen. Tech. Rep. PNW-635. Portland, OR: U.S. Department of Agriculture, Forest Service, Pacific Northwest Research Station: 107-118.

Kirkman, L.K; Coffey, K.L.; Mitchell, R J.; Moser, B. 2004. **Ground cover recovery patterns and life-history traits: implications for restoration obstacles and opportunities in a species rich savanna.** Journal of Ecology. 92: 409-421.

Kneeshaw, D.D.; Bergeron, Y. 1998. **Canopy gap characteristics and tree replacement in the southeastern boreal forest.** Ecology. 79: 782-795.

Knight, F.R. 1997. **A spatial analysis of a Sierra Nevada old-growth mixed-conifer forest.** Seattle, WA: University of Washington. 283 p. M.S. thesis.

Kohm, K.A.; Franklin, J.F. 1997. **Creating a forestry for the 21st century: the science of ecosystem management.** Washington, DC: Island Press. 491 p.

Kuusinen, M. 1994. **Epiphytic lichen diversity on *Salix caprea* in old-growth southern and middle boreal forests of Finland.** Annales Botanici Fennici. 31: 77-92.

Landres, P.B.; Morgan, P.; Swanson, F.J. 1999. **Overview of the use of natural variability concepts in managing ecological systems.** Ecological Applications. 9: 1179-1188.

Larson, A.J.; Franklin, J.F. 2005. **Patterns of conifer tree regeneration following an autumn wildfire event in the western Oregon Cascade Range, USA.** Forest Ecology and Management. 218: 25-36.

Leak, W.B. 1996. **Long-term structural change in uneven-aged northern hardwoods.** Forest Science. 42: 160-165.

Lertzman, K.P.; Sutherland, G.; Inselberg, A.; Saunders, S. 1996. **Canopy gaps and the landscape mosaic in a temperate rainforest.** Ecology. 77: 1254-1270.

Lindenmayer, D.B.; Franklin, J.F. 2002. **Conserving forest biodiversity: a comprehensive multi-scaled approach.** Washington, DC: Island Press, 352 p.

Lorimer, C.G.; Frelich, L.E. 1984. **A simulation of equilibrium diameter distributions of sugar maple (*Acer saccharum*).** Bulletin of the Torrey Botanical Club. 111: 193-199.

Lorimer C.G.; Dahir, S.E.; Nordheim, E.V. 2001. **Tree mortality rates and longevity in mature and old-growth hemlock-hardwood forests.** Journal of Ecology. 89: 960-971.

Louma, D.L.; Stockdale, C.A.; Molina, R.; Eberhart, J.L. 2006. **The spatial influence of *Pseudotsuga menziessi* retention trees on ectomycorrhiza diversity.** Canadian Journal of Forest Research. 36: 2561-2573.

Maser, C.; Tarrant, R.F.; Trappe, J.M.; Franklin, J.F. 1988. **From the forest to the sea: a story of fallen trees.** Gen. Tech. Rep. PNW-229. Portland, OR: U.S. Department of Agriculture, Forest Service, Pacific Northwest Forest and Range Experiment Station. 153 p.

Matthews, J.D. 1989. **Silvicultural systems.** Oxford: Oxford University Press. 285 p.

McGuire J.P.; Mitchell, R.J.; Moser, E.B.; Pecot, S.D.; Gjerstad, D.H.; Hedman, C.W. 2001. **Gaps in a gappy forest: plant resources, pine regeneration, and understory response to tree removal in longleaf pine savannas.** Canadian Journal of Forest Research. 31: 765-778.

McNulty, S.G.; Lorio, P.L., Jr.; Ayres, M.P.; Reeve, J.D. 1998. **Predictions of southern pine beetle populations using a forest ecosystem model.** In: Mickler, R.A.; Fox, S., eds. The productivity and sustainability of southern forest ecosystems in a changing environment. New York: Springer-Verlag: 617-634.

Michener, W. K.; Blood, E.R.; Box, J.B.; Couch, C.A.; Golladay, S.W.; Hippe, D.J.; Mitchell, R.J.; Palik, B.J. 1998. **Tropical storm flooding of a coastal plain landscape.** BioScience. 48: 696-705.

Mitchell, R.J.; Neel, W.L.; Hiers, J.K.; Cole, F.T.; Atkinson, J.B. 2000. **A model management plan for conservation easements in longleaf pine-dominated landscapes.** Newton, GA: Joseph W. Jones Ecological Research Center. 24 p.

Mitchell, S.J.; Beese, W.J. 2002. **The retention system: reconciling variable retention with the principles of silvicultural systems.** The Forestry Chronicle. 78: 397-403.

Monserud, R.A.; Sterba, H. 1999. **Modeling individual tree mortality for Austrian forest species.** Forest Ecology and Management. 113: 109-123.

Moser, W.K.; Jackson, S.M.; Podrazsky, V.; Larsen, D.R. 2002. **Examination of stand structure on quail plantations in the Red Hills region of Georgia and Florida managed by the Stoddard-Neel system: an example for forest managers.** Forestry. 75: 443-449.

Myers, R.K.; van Lear, D.H. 1998. **Hurricane-fire interactions in coastal forests of the south: a review and hypothesis.** Forest Ecology and Management. 103: 265-276.

Noel, J.M.; Platt, W.J.; Moser, E.B. 1998. **Structural characteristics of old- and second-growth stands of longleaf pine (*Pinus palustris*) in the Gulf Coastal Region of the U.S.A.** Conservation Biology. 12: 533-548.

Nyland, R.D. 2002. **Silviculture: concepts and application.** New York: McGraw-Hill. 624 p.

O'Hara, K.L. 1996. **Dynamics and stocking-level relationships of multi-aged ponderosa pine stands.** Forest Science Monograph. 42. 34 p.

O'Hara, K.L. 2001. **The silviculture transformation—a commentary.** Forest Ecology and Management. 151: 81-86.

Oliver, C.D.; Larson, B.C. 1996. **Forest stand dynamics.** New York: Wiley. 540 p.

Orr, P.W. 1963. **Windthrown timber survey in the Pacific Northwest, 1962.** Portland, OR: Insect and Disease Control Branch, Division of Timber Management, Pacific Northwest Region. 60 p.

Palik, B.J.; Pregitzer, K.S. 1991. **The relative influence of establishment time and height growth on species vertical stratification during secondary forest succession.** Canadian Journal of Forest Research. 21: 1760-1767.

Palik, B.J.; Pregitzer, K.S. 1993a. **The vertical development of early successional forests in northern Lower Michigan, USA.** Journal of Ecology. 81: 271-285.

Palik, B.J.; Pregitzer, K.S. 1993b. **The repeatability of stem exclusion during even-aged development of bigtooth aspen-dominated forests.** Canadian Journal of Forest Research. 23: 1156-1168.

Palik, B.J., Pregitzer, K. S. 1994. **White pine seed tree legacies in an aspen landscape: influences on post-disturbance white pine population structure.** Forest Ecology and Management. 67: 191-202.

Palik, B.J.; Pederson, N. 1996. **Natural disturbance and overstory mortality in longleaf pine ecosystems.** Canadian Journal of Forest Research. 26: 2035-2047.

Palik, B.J.; Engstrom, R.T. 1999. **Species composition.** In: Hunter, M.L., Jr., ed. Managing forests for biodiversity. New York: Cambridge University Press: 65-94.

Palik, B.J.; Robl, J. 1999. **Structural legacies of catastrophic windstorm in a mature Great Lakes** aspen forest. Res. Pap. NC-337. St. Paul, MN: U.S. Department of Agriculture, Forest Service, North Central Forest Experiment Station. 11 p.

Palik, B.J.; Mitchell, R.J.; Hiers, J. K. 2002. **Modeling silviculture after natural disturbance to maintain biological diversity: balancing complexity and implementation.** Forest Ecology and Management. 155: 347-356.

Palik, B.J.; Zasada, J. 2002. **An ecological context for regenerating multi-cohort, mixed-species red pine forests.** Res. Note NC-382. St. Paul, MN: U.S. Department of Agriculture, Forest Service, North Central Research Station. 8 p.

Palik, B.; Mitchell, R.J.; Pecot, S.; Battaglia, M.; Mou, P. 2003. **Spatial distribution of overstory retention influences resources and growth of longleaf pine seedlings.** Ecological Applications. 13: 674-686.

Palik, B.; Kern, C.; Mitchell, R.J.; Pecot, S. 2005. **Using spatially variable overstory retention to restore structural and compositional complexity in pine ecosystems.** Gen. Tech. Rep. PNW-635. In: Peterson, C.E.; Maguire, D.A., eds. Balancing ecosystem values: innovative experiments for sustainable forestry. Portland, OR: U.S. Department of Agriculture, Forest Service, Pacific Northwest Research Station: 285-290.

Parsons, W.F.J.; Knight, D.H.; Miller, S.L. 1994. **Root gap dynamics in a lodgepole pine forest, nitrogen transformations in gaps of different size.** Ecological Applications. 4: 354-362.

Pecore, M. 1992. **Menominee sustained yield management: a successful land ethic in practice.** Journal of Forestry. 90: 12-16.

Peterson, C.J.; Pickett, S.T.A. 1995. **Forest reorganization: a case study in an old-growth forest catastrophic blowdown.** Ecology. 76: 763-774.

Peterson, C.J. 2004. **Within-stand variation in windthrow in southern boreal forests of Minnesota,**

Is it predictable? Canadian Journal of Forest Research. 34: 365-375.

Pickett, S.T.A.; White, P.S., eds. 1985. **The ecology of natural disturbance and patch dynamics.** New York: Academic Press. 473 p.

Pimm, S.L.; Davis, G.E.; Loope, L.; Roman, C.T. 1994. **Hurricane Andrew.** BioScience. 44: 224-229.

Rebertus, A.J.; Williamson, G.B.; Moser, E.B. 1989. **Longleaf pine pyrogenicity and turkey oak mortality in Florida xeric sandhills.** Ecology. 70: 60-70.

Rebertus, A.J.; Kitzberger, T.; Veblen, T.T.; Roovers, L.M. 1997. **Blowdown history and landscape patterns in the Andes of Tierra del Fuego, Argentina.** Ecology. 78: 678-692.

Reich, P.B.; Bakken, P.; Carlson, D.; Frelich, L.E.; Friedman, S.K.; Grigal, D.F. 2001. **Influence of logging, fire, and forest type on biodiversity and productivity in southern boreal forests.** Ecology. 82: 2731-2748.

Romme, W.H.; Knight, D.H. 1981. **Fire frequency and subalpine forest succession along a topographic gradient in Wyoming.** Ecology. 62: 319-326.

Romme, W.H.; Knight, D.H.; Yavitt, J.B. 1986. **Mountain pine beetle outbreaks in the Rocky Mountains: regulators of primary productivity?** American Naturalist. 127: 484-494.

Runkle, J.R. 1982. **Patterns of disturbance in some old-growth mesic forests of eastern North America.** Ecology. 63: 1533-1546.

Runkle, J.R. 1998. **Changes in southern Appalachian canopy tree gaps sampled thrice.** Ecology. 79: 1768-1780.

Seymour, R.S.; Hunter, M.L., Jr. 1999. **Principles of ecological forestry.** In: Hunter, M.L., Jr., ed.

Composition in managing forests for biodiversity. New York: Cambridge University Press: 22-61.

Seymour, R.S.; White, A.S.; deMaynadier, P.G. 2002. **Natural disturbance regimes in northeastern North America—evaluating silvicultural systems using natural scales and frequencies.** Forest Ecology and Management. 155: 357-367.

Seymour, R.S.; Guldin, J.; Marshall, D.; Palik, B. 2006. **Large-scale, long-term silvicultural experiments in the United States: historical overview and contemporary examples.** Allgemeine Forst Und Jagdseitung. 177: 104-112.

Sharpe, G.W. 1956. **A taxonomical-ecological study of vegetation by habitats in eight forest types of the Olympic Rain Forest, Olympic National Park, Washington.** Seattle, WA: University of Washington. 165 p. Ph.D. thesis.

Simberloff, D. 1999. **The role of science in the preservation of biodiversity.** Forest Ecology and Management. 115: 101-111.

Smith, D.M.; Larson, B.C.; Kelty, M.J.; Ashton, P.M.S. 1996. **The practice of silviculture: applied forest ecology, 9th ed.** New York: John Wiley and Sons. 560 p.

Spies, T.A.; Franklin, J.F.; Thomas, T.B.; 1988. **Coarse woody debris in Douglas-fir forests of western Oregon and Washington.** Ecology. 69: 1689-1702.

Spies, T.A.; Franklin, J.F. 1991. **The structure of natural young, mature, and old-growth Douglas-fir forests in Oregon and Washington.** In: Ruggiero, L.F.; Aubry, K.B.; Carey, A.B.; Huff, M.H., eds. Wildlife and vegetation of unmanaged Douglas-fir forests. Gen. Tech. Rep. PNW-285. Portland, OR: U.S. Department of Agriculture, Forest Service, Pacific Northwest Forest and Range Experiment Station: 91-109.

Strong, T.F.; Teclaw, R.M.; Zasada, J.C. 1997. **Monitoring the effects of partial cutting and gap size on microclimate and vegetation responses in northern hardwood forests in Wisconsin.** Gen. Tech. Rep. NC-238. St. Paul, MN: U.S.Department of Agriculture, Forest Service, North Central Forest Experiment Station. 12 p.

Tappeiner, J.C.; Huffman, D.; Marshall, D.; Spies, T.A.; Bailey, J.D. 1997. **Density, ages, and growth rates in old-growth and young-growth forests in coastal Oregon.** Canadian Journal of Forest Research. 27: 638-648.

Turner, M.G.; Baker, W.L.; Peterson, C.J.; Peet, R.K. 1998. **Factors influencing succession: lessons from large, infrequent natural disturbances.** Ecosystems. 1: 511-523.

USDA Forest Service. 2004. **Chequamegon-Nicolet National Forest Final Forest Plan** (2004 Land and Resource Management Plan). 670 p.

Vanha-Majamaa, I.; Jalonen, J. 2001. **Green tree retention in Fennoscandian forestry.** Scandinavian Journal of Forest Research Supplement. 3: 79-90.

Van Wagner, C.E. 1971. **Fire and red pine.** In: Proceedings of the 10th annual Tall Timbers fire ecology conference. Tallahassee, FL: Tall Timbers Research Station: 211-219.

Veblen, T.T.; Hadley, K.S.; Reid, M.S.; Rebertus, A.J. 1991. **The response of subalpine forests to spruce beetle outbreak in Colorado.** Ecology. 72: 213-231.

Verner, J.; McKelvey, K.S; Noon, B.R.; Gutierrez, R.J.: Gould, G.I., Jr.; Beck, T.W. 1992. **The California spotted owl: a technical assessment of its current status.** Gen. Tech. Rep. PSW-133. Berkeley, CA: U.S. Department of Agriculture, Forest Service, Pacific Southwest Forest and Range Experiment Station. 285 p.

Wahlenburg, W.G. 1946. **Longleaf pine: its use, ecology, regeneration, protection, growth, and management.1st ed.** Washington, DC: Charles Lathrop Pack Forestry Foundation, 256 p.

Walker, L.R.; Brokaw, N.V.L.; Lodge, D.J.; Waide, R.B. eds. 1991. **Special issue: Ecosystem, plant, and animal responses to hurricanes in the Caribbean.** Biotropica. 23: 313-521.

Williamson, G.B.; Black, E.M. 1981. **High temperature of forest fires under pines as a selective advantage over oaks.** Nature. 293: 643-644.

Williamson, R.L. 1982. **Response to commercial thinning in a 110-year-old Douglas-fir stand.** Res. Pap. PNW-296. Portland, OR: U.S. Department of Agriculture, Forest Service, Pacific Northwest Forest and Range Experiment Station. 16 p.